JOHN GALT
Reappraisals

John Galt from an oil painting by Joshua Smith, R.B.A. This painting was presented to the City of Guelph by the descendants of John Galt on April 23rd, 1927, in honour of their centenary celebrations.

JOHN GALT
Reappraisals

edited by
Elizabeth Waterston

with best wishes,
March 26, 1988
Elizabeth Waterston

University of Guelph
1985

ISBN 0-920512-06- 2.
The University of Guelph,
Guelph, Ontario,
Canada. N1G 2W1
Printed and bound in Canada by Ampersand Printing,
Guelph, Ontario.

CONTENTS

Preface

The occasion for these reappraisals of John Galt was a conference held in Guelph, Ontario, in June 1984. Speaking in this Ontario University city, which has grown from Galt's Upper Canadian settlement, several commentators focused on Galt's work here, and particularly on *Bogle Corbet,* the fictional version of Galt's life in Guelph. In consequence, the contents of this volume balance, without any advance intention of doing so, the coverage in the last major collection of essays on Galt: *John Galt, 1779 - 1979,* edited by C.A.Whatley (Edinburgh: Ramsay Head, 1979).

Our reappraisals do not concentrate, as that earlier collection did, on *Annals of the Parish, Ringan Gilhaize* or *The Entail;* we do draw attention to *The Last of the Lairds* and *The Ayrshire Legatees,* as well as to Galt's New World novels, and we offer new light on Galt as politician and as urban planner.

Let us hope that another five years will produce yet another Galt conference, and yet another resultant book of essays to enrich the pleasure of all readers who enjoy the work of John Galt!

The Guelph conference started, as this volume does, with a contribution by Erik Frykman of Goteborg, Sweden. Professor Frykman began by reminiscing about his time at Aberdeen, in the days when he moved into Galt scholarship, trying to assess Galt's knowledge of the Scottish Common Sense Philosophy, to examine local records of the West of Scotland to see whether they confirmed or contradicted Galt's social pictures, and generally to explore the early Galt period. Having reminded a sympathetic audience of early days in modern Galt research, Professor Frykman turned to those Galt books which were outside his original range of interest, the New World novels, *Lawrie Todd* and *Bogle Corbet.* For his reminiscences, his paper, and his genial contributions to the Guelph discussion, we can apply to Dr. Frykman the phrase he uses about Galt: "There is every reason to remember him with respect and affection."

Gilbert Stelter, of the Department of History, University of Guelph, made a dramatic revelation of a new reason for us to respect John Galt. Professor Stelter's recent discovery of a long-lost plan drawn up as a design for Guelph proves the sensitivity and modernity of Galt as "booster and builder" of urban centrism. The obliteration of the plan illustrates the kind of bad luck that seemed to dog Galt. Professor Stelter adds however a historical perspective in which Galt seems justified, ultimately, by "logic, experience and history"

Annotation of a passage of Galt's autobiography presented by Nicholas Whistler clarifies the modification of facts in Galt's memoirs of his days as townbuilder in Guelph. The *Autobiography* remains the most important work by Galt not readily available in a modern reissue. We all look forward to seeing it in print some time soon.

Bogle Corbet — or at least the final third of that novel — has been available since 1977 in the New Canadian Library edition. I now add to my comments in the "Introduction" to that volume some further ideas about *Bogle Corbet,* Galt's ideas on town life, and the influence of these ideas on subsequent Canadian fiction.

Conversely, the next paper in this collection looks at elements in *Bogle Corbet* which extend an earlier literary style — that of the sentimental romance, so popular a survival from the days of Mackenzie's *Man of Feeling.* Martin Bowman, of Champlain Regional College, Quebec, played a valuable informative part in discussions at the Guelph conference; we are glad to add a contribution from an energetic young Canadian scholar to this volume.

The focus on *Bogle Corbet* ends, and we turn to another examination of Galt as extending and improving an earlier convention. Keith Costain of the University of Regina, the best known of Canadian critics of Galt, here analyzes *The Ayrshire Legatees* as an epistolary novel. This important essay demonstrates the complexity of Galt's intentions and achievements, and adds a new dimension of understanding to one of the best-loved of the novels.

The Last of the Lairds is the subject of another careful analysis, this time by Hans de Groot, of the University of Toronto. Dr. de Groot draws our attention to the ingenious use of a narrator who is peripheral to the story, yet who is subtly and importantly changed by his observation of its events.

The general theme of chance and change, as considered by Ian Campbell of the University of Edinburgh, widened the focus of the conference from particular techniques to an intellectual overview. Dr. Campbell's criticism over the past decades has helped define Galt's place in the mainstream of Scottish fiction. He comments here on the way Galt's characters develop in the reader's mind. Dr. Campbell's comments on Galt's "triumphant achievements" capped our growing awareness of the strengths of the author we had gathered to celebrate.

"A man of formidable talent", said Ian Gordon, dean of the Galt circle. Professor Gordon, who equals Galt in energy, pulled together five political novels, two hemispheres, and two John Galts in one penetrating examination. Over the years, Professor Gordon has stacked edition after edition of Galt's novels and short stories beside his own definitive biography; at the conference, to the incisive essay published here he added a memorable banquet address.

The Guelph conference is over; the essays remain as a recapturing of a pleasurable and profitable symposium. For the success of that June experience, we all acknowledge our indebtedness to the Social Sciences and Humanities

Research Council of Canada, which provided financial support; to Professor Earl MacNaughton, co-ordinator of the Conference of Learned Societies of Canada at Guelph, who facilitated arrangements; to indefatigable Nick Whistler, who organized the sessions, the workshop, and the banquet; and to Dean David Murray, who proffered the hospitality of the College of Arts, University of Guelph. It is also a pleasure to thank Dr. B.C. Matthews, President of the University of Guelph, who facilitated the production of this volume.

Elizabeth Waterston,
Guelph, Ontario,
January, 1985.

John Galt's new world novels

Erik Frykman

I have never held the view that because you like and admire an author you must blind yourself to his artistic shortcomings, and in the case of Galt this is hardly possible. I should think it must be a generally shared view that his ambitions led him astray on more than one occasion and that, poor man, in some phases of his life assiduous scribbling was a way to make both ends if possible meet. What I wish to consider now is this: is there anything in *Lawrie Todd* and *Bogle Corbet* that we haven't met with in Galt's earlier works, particularly in the earlier first-person stories like *Annals of the Parish* and *The Provost?* Is it possible to speak of a development of narrative method, thematic content and outlook? The questions can be put in a different way: What kinship is there between these two novels and the earlier stories? I shall deal with the novels in turn, in the case of *Bogle Corbet* concentrating almost entirely on the Canadian part.

What is definitely new is, of course, the setting. It is not for me to even try to guess at Galt's success in giving a convincing and comprehensive account of the circumstances in which the emigrants and settlers of the period found themselves, and the problems they had to cope with. My own impression is that he managed to bring in a good deal and to interweave the life-story of an individual and the background in a way that does not show the effort too obviously. On the other hand, at least as far as *Lawrie Todd* is concerned, even though there is a good deal of recording of social fact there seems to be less of thoughts and ideas about social change and social ideals than in the *Annals*. What there is is not absolutely consistent. At one point trade is thought of as an ever-fluctuating and thus unrewarding pursuit compared with farming; (I, 149f.)[1] but in fact, Lawrie admits that it is the successful combination of both that makes for his rise to wealth and social influence. (I, 218).

The life-story itself could be summarized as a rise attended by contrarieties, at points also by misgivings and personal sorrow, but with confidence and determination renewed and ultimate comfort and content attained. Lawrie's story is most nearly akin to Andrew Wylie's in that it is a success gained against heavy odds — or perhaps rather, against personal oddity, but an oddity that both of them know how to turn into account. The difference is, of course, that in the case of Lawrie Galt could not provide an aristocratic family for his protagonist to serve as rough-diamond helper and adviser to; which is just as well since that part of *Sir Andrew Wylie* is not one of Galt's narrative triumphs.

Why did he choose to make Lawrie a Midlothian Scot? Was it just in order to avoid repetition, a feeling that he had worked out the West Country mine? No, I think there may have been another reason, which becomes noticeable in the part of the story where Lawrie returns for a while to his native land: he makes some hits there at East Country genteelness, off-setting it against Lawrie's own humble origins, no doubt also against the general democratic spirit among the settlers. In a wider context Galt is anxious to put Europe in its place in comparison with America: Lawrie finds that in many respects his native Scotland is lagging behind in the matter of "improvements" (III, 5). But here as elsewhere — and this I think is characteristic of Galt as a writer — he strikes a balance and does not simplify unduly. This is true also of his picture of North American social life: there may be greater equality, but there is also a good deal of competition and manoeuvering and no absolute absence of social prestige and snobbism.

As in *Annals of the Parish* and *The Provost* the narrator has both a small circle of friends and some vexatious antagonists. At one end of the scale of Lawrie's friends is the rough-and ready Mr. Hoskins, Lawrie's second father-in-law, an outspoken and canny man who in spite of brief appearances only is convincingly portrayed. At the other end is Mrs. Cockspur, "a lady of settees and wax-candles" (II, 105), refined without being snobbishly genteel; socially a cut above Mrs. Malcolm in *Annals of the Parish* but like her providing the narrator and his family with suitably polite company.

Among the unforgettable scenes in the *Annals* are Mr. Balwhidder's confrontations with Lady Macadam and the irascible Mr. Cayenne. The subtlety of Galt's psychological insight in such scenes, the way in which he makes the Minister unconsciously reveal his pride in his own resourcefulness, is truly admirable. He repeated such performances, amusingly enough but less subtly, I feel, in Mr. Pawkie's dealings with his adversaries in *The Provost.* The pattern is continued in *Lawrie Todd,* but alas, that ubiquitous aggravating creature Bailie Waft becomes just tedious. The mutual outwitting process going on between him and Lawrie might have been entertaining if Galt had known how to economize, as he did so admirably in the *Annals;* but Waft is brought in by hook or by crook on every imaginable occasion and none of the numerous episodes in which he figures has much point.

However, the really painful episode in the novel — and a protracted one at that — is the incident with the anxious-to-get-married spinster in vol. II, a piece of sheer, tasteless padding, a low-watermark of Galtian humour. When an author has to assure the reader that the characters involved in a supposedly funny situation have fits of uncontrollable laughter at somebody's expense, then there is definitely something wrong.

Let it be said, however, to restore the balance, that even though the novel shows clear marks of Galt's usual difficulty in spinning out a story, there are on the other hand a number of well-told scenes and incidents; and let it be added to Galt's credit also that as in the earlier phase of his literary career he was capable of conveying pathos with restraint and without mawkishness. The manner in which Lawrie is made to narrate the death of his two children offers good examples, and also the incident at an early stage of the story where a river in spate destroys the first hut that Lawrie had just put up for himself and his family. An excellent example of Galt's power of subdued pathos — recognizable from his early books — is the description of the way life in the raw goes on as usual during the ravages of the yellow fever in New York, a passage reminiscent of Defoe though I do not believe it is a case of imitation:

> But there were cumpunctionless men amongst us whom nothing at that feast of death could daunt from their orgies. One beautiful moonlight evening, towards the end of September, I walked up Broadway, mourning for the desolation around. I stopped near the spot in Chamber-street where the man in other times used to fix his telescope to look at the moon: I felt as if I then stood on the line between the living and the dead. Below was the stillness of death, only interrupted now and then by the groans of the sick and the dying, and the rattling of the slow-coming hearse. Above was the usual bustle of street-walkers; and the wind blowing gently from the north, I could plainly distinguish the blasphemous mirth of a crowd at the door of the circus, whose interior was filled with citizens who had but lately fled from death. The sound was to my ear as rottenness to the smell; it was as the neighings of Gomorrah. (I, 69f.)

How well-planned in advance the novel may have been is impossible to say; but certain passages show that Galt must have become aware that a variety of different kinds of scenes and incidents were called for. At one point, for instance, he makes Lawrie say that the reader's patience must not be overtaxed by too detailed an account of his business dealings. Clearly as the story progressed Galt felt the need of including dramatic matter other than that provided by epidemics, forest fires, floodings and perilous expeditions into the backwoods. Hence the rambling recapitulation of Mrs. Cockspur's and her wooer Mr. Herbert's past, hence also the spinster incident and the story of Lawrie's son. The lad is sent to New York to learn book-keeping and gets into bad company. He ends up badly wounding an adversary in a duel, so that he has to flee the country. He escapes to Scotland and is taken loving care of by his grandfather. What is particularly noticeable in this incident is that Galt makes Lawrie tell it with a good deal of parental understanding.

He is less fortunate with the story of Mr. Bell the clergyman, at least in its totality. He creates a moving scene out of the man's misery and shame caused by a wife who has taken to the bottle (and who is made to suffer a suitably horrid death by drowning). But the later incident of Bell's mental derangement and his attempt to push Lawrie into the foaming river becomes slightly ludicrous. At times Galt was also capable of careless execution of an incident: on one occasion one of Lawrie's sons fails to return home from a lonely expedition into the forest. A rescue party is sent out, including Lawrie himself, and they get into difficulties told at some length. What happened to the young man in the end is totally forgotten about. Could it be that Galt aimed at underscoring Lawrie's self-centredness? I doubt it, because such pointers are normally made explicit.

Apart from the social picture and the account of Lawrie's career the main interest in the novel is in the psychological portrait of the narrator — a repetition, in other words, of the pattern established in the *Annals* and *The Provost*. Lawrie is, of course, more nearly akin to Mr. Pawkie than to Mr. Balwhidder. Like the Provost, he is an endlessly projecting and scheming character, with an undeniable eye to the main chance but anxious also to serve the community. Like his predecessors he is quite capable of telling jokes against himself and, in fact, the story is set going in that spirit: in his young days,at the time of the French Revolution, he had been a demonstrating Radical and had been laughed to scorn by onlookers in Edinburgh because of his insignificant stature and other bodily handicaps. One suspects that Galt may have taken this opportunity to assure the authorities of his own political reliability.

Contrary to Mr. Balwhidder Lawrie characterizes himself explicitly: he is gifted, he says, with a courageous spirit, zeal of emulation, mother wit, brave confidence in himself and natural jocosity (I, 15, 17, 19 and 83); "a man of common sense and sedate reason" he also calls himself (II, 92).

Mr. Balwhidder — always, I think, the model of psychological revelation in the totality of Galt's oeuvre — is certainly proud of his own role and feels that he has a natural special position; and how skilfully Galt brings out this harmless pride! The robustious Mr. Pawkie has no hesitation in revealing his own importance. In the case of Lawrie Galt has been less fortunate: if one may borrow a Shakespearean phrase in a different sense, there is damnable iteration of Lawrie's assurances to the reader that Providence was on his side, and there are rather too many cases of self-gratulation, both on account of his own success and of what he does for others. Particularly in the early parts of the novel Lawrie is also too obviously pleased with the discomfiture of others, for instance the wealthy young man who has been courting the girl who prefers poor hard-working, much less prepossessing Lawrie instead. But, of course, Galt is far from alone in the period in perpetrating that kind of narrative sin.

It should be said on the other hand that Lawrie has a feeling for people in distress and that he shows great fairness to, and appreciation of, others — even at times of his particular pain in the neck, Bailie Waft. Again here Galt follows the pattern he had set in *Annals of the Parish* and which I think is an indication of his own character: he was not easily impressed, he spotted ridiculous and at times odious qualities in people, but he was also tolerant and appreciative.

"It is an infirmity of my nature to take an attachment to everything I happen to grow familiar with," says Lawrie (II, 249F.). However, even though this positive attitude is underlined by Galt, Lawrie's most conspicuous characteristic is his practicality, and it is most amusingly brought out when he seems unaware of the effect created, as in the description of the precautions he took on the occasion of a fire in New York:

> Having for many months previous resolved in my own mind how I should act when the event should take place, I was prepared and composed. My wife being dressed, I bade her carry the sick child to a place of safety, saying, that I would wake up and take care of the other children and servants. In the mean time I calmly but quickly dressed myself, and with considerate presence of mind I put on a pair of old double-soled boots, lest in the confusion I should tread on a rusty nail in some of the boards that might be pulled down: I then wetted my night-cap and put it on to preserve my hair from being singed, and having sent off the children and servants, I went down to my store, and secured my valuable papers and money, pinning them in my jacket pocket. (I, 100)

His matter-of-factness is at times devastating. His first marriage is one of mutual affection; numbers two and three entirely matters of egotistical convenience and careful calculation. The motto of the chapter that follows immediately on the account of his second wife's death is "Now let's to business" (II, 28), and the admission is made that "there was less missing of my wife than could have been thought possible" (II, 35). As for wife no. 3, a Scottish widow considerably younger than Lawrie himself, he makes it clear to her that "the first duty of a wedded wife consists in smoothing the pillow of her husband" (II, 93). Galt at this late stage of the story says good-bye to all psychological credibility: ". . . as she is still alive, I need not be in any haste in giving her a character, for she may yet change: I speak of her thus favourably, to encourage her in well-doing" (III, 107)."

The question arises as to Galt's own stance with regard to Lawrie's person and career. Is he in fact satirically and critically inclined? The fact that Lawrie is made to suffer some discomfiture at the hands of Bailie Waft makes it seem likely that, even if Galt wants the reader to admire Lawrie's pluck and initiative, he somehow wanted to establish a counterpoise. There are other and clearer indications also that Galt meant to convey a divided attitude to his hero. At an early stage Lawrie learns the lesson that "the cunning of man" is not what really makes for success (I, 116), and he admits to folly and lack of perspicacity about himself. Towards the end, although he calls himself "untarnished in my integrity" (III, 11), he thinks back to the early days in New York, when he was struggling along with his first wife in mutual affection, and cannot help feeling now that "the gathering of gear makes the heart sordid" (III, 90).

It seems to me likely that Galt wrote this novel in an ambivalent mood: there was probably some wishful thinking embedded in the story of Lawrie's attainment of success and esteem; but, because Galt had not achieved either, he represented such success and the striving for it as somewhat questionable.

To sum up: apart from the setting and the kind of adventure and hardship met with by settlers in an unknown country, I don't think there is really anything in the novel that can be termed a new departure. It is noticeable also that Galt is sparing in his use of Scotticisms, as if he were afraid that such things might not be pleasing to a prospective English public and to the governmental authorities. The careful balancing he had maintained in his earlier stories in providing for the interest of both Scottish and English readers is less in evidence here. It is true that he makes his protagonist a Scotsman and surrounds him with some other Scottish settlers in the New World; on the other hand, the section of the novel that is set in Scotland does not seem particularly adapted to the purpose of creating sympathy for the book there.

What then about *Bogle Corbet?* If Galt had proved unable or unwilling to deviate from earlier patterns in *Lawrie Todd,* is it likely that, with increasing burdens on his mind, he should have been able to create something new a short time afterwards? Curiously enough, I think this is so.

From the outset Bogle describes himself as "a very ordinary man" (I, 1), but a man anxious to preserve a maximum of independence, "not greatly susceptible," he says, "of impressions from others" (I, 52). The story of his career is pretty dry — you could also choose to say that it has a sobriety of tone unmarred by the kind of jocosity that can at times be a little trying in *Lawrie Todd.* I have little doubt that in a discreet way Galt wrote this book as a story about himself, in the light of his failure to achieve what he may have hoped for: "What blind things we are! and how common it is among the young to imagine themselves better qualified for other pursuits than those in which they are engaged..." (I, 271).

In some respects *Bogle Corbet* is no doubt a rather shocking affair. The Canadian part in itself is a mishmash, part factual account of a settler's life, part travelogue, part an attempt at fictionalization, and, to end it all, that well-known piece of factual padding, his practical information about various districts of Upper Canada. What novelistic fiction there is concerns the discovery of blood relationship between two people and the story of a fortunate inheritance, trite motifs of the period not very excitingly told.

But the book has other qualities, particularly straightforward, unsentimental recording of facts and opinions and, added to that, at times a resigned tone which strikes me as new for Galt.[2] Here and there there are also some rather fine descriptions of scenery.

The observations of the Governmental authorities are few but to the point: the narrator accuses the mother country of a "negligent colonial system" — "if system it can be called" (II, 306). The majority of immigrants, in their turn, are accused of importunity, restlessness and unwillingness to cooperate, though Galt is also anxious to point to praiseworthy exceptions. As elsewhere, including *Lawrie Todd,* Galt has little time for religious sectarianism: "the most rigid of the righteous amongst us had no cause to moan for lack of Gospel fodder," is Bogle's terse remark on the emergence of preachers of different denominations (III, 259). He has some amusing pages about people who wax lyrical about their impression of the Niagara Falls: "my waterfall-days are pretty well over," says Bogle (III, 216), and Mrs. Bogle is if anything even less enthusiastic. Bogle's relationship with his wife is the subject of a few thrown-out hints only. "The logical arrangement of Mrs. Corbet's ideas was never of the strictest sort," says her husband (III, 186), and there is a passage which recalls to one's mind Mr. Balwhidder's slightly melancholy account of the untiring domestic economy of the second Mrs. Balwhidder, which turned him into a rather solitary man. This is what Bogle says:

To say nothing of pigs and sheep to kill, and joints to send to obliging neighbours who had remembered us in similar operations, sausages to stuff and yarn to bleach and worsted to dye; we had quilting beds, upholstery jobs, and, in short, more various manufactures in hand than would have served for the supply of any ten decent families in the old country. This bustle often interfered with our comfort; and yet, though it was the evident heart's delight of Mrs. Corbet to be stirring in hot water of her own boiling, the more she had to do the less was she content, and gave vent to the most pathetic complaints concerning her turmoils, telling me that her "bit and her drop were dearly bought," adding with a sigh, "it would come to an end;" and whenever I responded amen, which I did on every occasion with perfect sincerity, she would accuse me of being destitute of sympathy. (III, 174-5)

Galt was reticent about his own marriage. Whatever the relation between fact and fiction in this respect may have been, there is a tone of noticeable sadness in Bogle's account of his own life at this stage, in striking contrast to the indomitable spirit of Lawrie Todd. There are a couple of eloquently described domestic scenes which are realistic in their picture of listlessness, isolation, and occasional physical discomforts, for instance this:

These sort of hardships, though almost ludicrous in the recital, were yet grievous in the experience. They did not, it is true, frequently occur, but often enough to do more than molest our comfort; and the worst of them consisted in making the younger children querulous and importunate to be taken home; which, though a childish longing, became sometimes exceedingly distressing; for the poor creatures, after fretting and complaining, would subside into sadness, and sit apart and moan to themselves with so much of the accent of desertion, that their mother often said it was more pitiful to hear them than if they were Babes in the Wood, and she herself a tender-hearted Robin Redbreast. But as the winter wore away, custom, with its wonted conciliation, mitigated our sufferings, and many things which at their first occurrence were severe evils, came to be pass without observation. (III, 147-8)

Or take another example:

Our view, not extensive, is circumscribed by the woods; not another dwelling is in sight, nor for several miles accessible; no post brings even an afflicting letter. The newspaper of last week has been already read all over, advertisments and all, a score of times. The faculties of the mind are relaxed; not a book is worth reading. It requires fine weather, a frosty night, and a bright fire, to discover the genius of Shakspeare. Our hearth is piled with splintering pine, and it would be cruel to make the servant look for better in the wood-shed on such a night as this. The children quarrel, they know not wherefore; Mrs. Corbet has a box not opened till to-day since we left London; moths may have got into the clothes, its contents are spread abroad, and sure enough a mouse has made a nest in the corner, and has three young ones — all is deplorable. I sit by the fire thinking unutterable things, and saying to myself, this is life and the pleasure of mine for all my days, — heigh ho! (III, 115-6)

Galt would not be Galt, however, if he did not let a narrator protagonist speak in positive terms about his life; but it is noticeable that when Bogle makes his summing-up, it is not entirely free of a note of disappointment:

But why should I thus speak of the world, wherein I have received so much indulgence, and merely because, perhaps, I may have been justified in feeling sentiments of resentment against individuals? To the general world I can have no antipathy; it has been always my generous and disinterested friend; when those particular persons, on whom I might have better accounted, showed themselves wanting, the general world towards me has been ever kind. I rejoice that I have uniformly been towards it of that mind; but I regret to have discerned, that individuals to whom I have surrendered confidence, have repaid me with ingratitude. (III, 58)

One must, as usual, take care not to equate life and fictional account; but it does not seem entirely unlikely that on this occasion Galt is speaking for and about himself. If so, one feels sadness on his account. No doubt he had made his mistakes in life, no doubt he had been over-confident in his own powers and lacking in discretion. But he had also achieved something in literature, possibly more also in colonial enterprise than the authorities were willing to give him credit for. There is every reason to remember him with respect and affection.

NOTES

[1]References to the novels, within brackets in the text, are to *Lawrie Todd; or, The Settlers in the Woods.* Second Edition. (London: Colburn and Bentley, 1830) and to *Bogle Corbet, or, the Emigrants.* (London: Colburn and Bentley, 1831).

[2]This has been admirably noted by Professor Waterston in her introduction to the paperback edition of *Bogle Corbet* (Toronto: McClelland and Stewart, 1977, p.7): "He |Galt| paints, also, the streaks on a human heart: the shades of depression, melancholy, irritation, ironic self-deprecation." Critical insights into sides of Galt's genius other than the pawkily humorous and the socially descriptive are indeed welcome.

John Galt: The writer as town booster and builder

Gilbert A. Stelter

"So you see, if you tell me of books," John Galt wrote a friend in Scotland in 1828," I can tell you of new towns – and which are the most interesting I leave Christopher North and the Shepherd to determine."[1] Galt was in a unique position to judge the relative merits of writing and town founding; an established author, he had published more than a dozen books of fiction, biography and travel before founding the towns of Guelph and Goderich in the Upper Canadian wilderness. He felt that North – the pseudonym of John Wilson, professor of moral philosophy at the University of Edinburgh and the main editorial force behind *Blackwood's Edinburgh Magazine* – and the Ettrick Shepherd, James Hogg, a country poet, would be able to appreciate both the literary and business sides of his career. These two sides were much more closely connected than most recent observers seem to realize.[2]

Galt himself was blunt about the place of writing in his life: "I. . . never regarded my books but as Hogarth did his portraits, viz pot boilers."[3] Even in the book summing up his literary career he wrote that he had "ever held literature to be a secondary pursuit. . . but when my numerous books are forgotten, I should yet be remembered. . . I contrived the Canada Company, which will hereafter be spoken of among the eras of a nation destined to greatness."[4] Galt's Canadian achievements were far less important than he judged them to be, but his perspective was significant. He represented what really amounted to a commercial approach to the question of how Canada should be settled, in contrast to the previously prevailing emphasis on the imperial government's direction and subsidization. He would not have regarded J.G. Lockhart's characterization of him "as having had the Education and habits of a merchant" as an insult.[5] From his boyhood as the son of a shipmaster in the westcoast Scottish seaport of Irvine, and his youth in the bustling port of Greenock, Galt was closely associated with commerce and especially with international trade and shipping. When, at the age of twenty-five in 1804, he left his clerk's position in a mercantile firm he did so with the hopes of a great business career although he had developed a talent for producing some pretty turgid Gothic epic poetry.[6]

For the next twenty-two years Galt pursued a series of unsuccessful business ventures in Britain and Europe. He also travelled extensively in the Mediterranean countries and Asia Minor, always on the lookout for commercial possibilities. The vagaries of fortune prompted repeated moves between London and Scotland. His business connections with Canada began in 1820 when he was sought out as a lobbyist at Westminister for a group of Upper Canadians who were claiming compensation for losses as a result of the war with the Americans from 1812-1815. While that effort at persuading officialdom became sidetracked in complications, his discussions with government officials on matters of colonial land sales and emigration gave birth to the idea of a colonizing venture and the complex political and commercial negotiations leading to the foundation of the Canada company. But a lack of sufficient income was always a central feature of his life, and a good deal of his writing was done strictly to provide a modicum of respectability for himself and his growing family. He was able to pour out a tremendous volume of material during these years, ranging from journalistic essays, and text books for children to well researched biographies of Cardinal Wolsey and Benjamin West, and some of his best ficition, which he called theoretical histories, not novels, such as *The Ayrshire Legatees* (1820), *Annals of the Parish* (1821), *The Provost* (1822), *Andrew Wylie* (1822), *The Entail* (1823), and *The Last of the Lairds* (1826).

The total body of Galt's writing, including his fiction, provides a unique insight into the perceptions and thoughts of a central actor in some of the most significant social processes in the early nineteenth century. Galt was very much interested in the nature of urban development wherever he travelled, and also in the way towns played a key role in the settlement process in the new world. These ideas were already developed before he actually had the opportunity to become a town planner and builder. They were refined during the relatively short period of practical experience in Upper Canada from late 1826 to early 1829. And they were reflected on for another decade as he tried to justify his Canadian performance. In the following pages I will outline Galt's perception of urban growth and expansion and then show how these were put into practise in his "great experiment."

Perceptions of Urbanism and Urban Growth

Galt shared with the Enlightenment the belief in progress and improvement.[7] The growth of towns and cities was a central feature of economic and cultural advance and social order. He generally accepted Adam Smith's view that "it is thus through the greater part of Europe the commerce and manufactures of cities, instead of being the effect, have been the cause and occasion of the improvement and cultivation of the country."[8] Smith had outlined three ways in which urban places affected the country positively: they offered a ready market for country produce; merchants bought land and improved it; order and good government were introduced. The darker side of urbanization was not as apparent to Galt as it would be to observers in the 1830s and 1840s when the industrial city was regarded as a threat to society as exemplified by the

London of Dickens or the Manchester of Engels. Galt's vision of the city was perhaps less penetrating than that of later observers, but it reflected an optimistic, commercial age before the negative consequences of industrialization had forged a new kind of urban consciousness, the idea of the city as vice, replacing the 18th century notion of the city as virtue.[9]

A remarkably clear perception of the character and function of urban places permeates much of Galt's writing. Because of his continuous travel he had occasion to visit and closely observe communities in several different societies and the narrators in much of his fiction are given the role of travellers to these same places. What emerges from his writing is a strong sense of systematic urban hierarchy headed by a great metropolis; cities as regional leaders; towns as active commercial centers; and finally the village, which he tends to equate with the country. His travellers are also sensitive to how behavior differed at each level of the hierarchy.

The most carefully delineated village in his works is Dalmailing in *Annals of the Parish.* Galt later wrote that he got the image from the village of Innerkip, near Greenock, where "some progress had been made by Sir John Shaw Stewart in turning it inside out," but that the setting of the book was actually Dreghorn, within sight of Irvine, his birthplace.[10] The village represents traditional and simple ways of life which are threatened by the building of a new cotton-mill town, Cayenneville, in the same parish. Galt's narrator, the parish minister, recognized "a new genius. . .that was not to be satisfied with the taciturn regularity of ancient affairs" and he soon "began to discover signs of decay in the wonted simplicity of our country ways."[11] The impact of this new industrial town was also felt in the political sphere, for those in Cayenneville "were afflicted with the itch of Jacobinism; but those of the village were staunch and true to king and country."[12] And finally, the new activity also resulted in the introduction of an inn into the village itself, bringing "as it were, the evil practices of towns into the heart of the country."[13]

The town of Irvine appears as Garnock in *The Ayrshire Legatees* and as Gudetown in *The Provost,* but the town he knew best as an adult was Greenock. His several periods of residency there were usually unhappy times "for there were no evening amusements. . .and as to visiting under the cloud of night, it was foreign to the customs of the place."[14] And so he generally satirized what he felt was Greenock's excessively high regard for its cultural status, as in suggesting that the town had been "so justly, for its taste in the fine arts, denominated the Florence of the West."[15] As to Greenock's economic pretensions, he put forward the following nonsensical logic as perhaps typical of their thinking about

> the metropolitan town which Greenock certinly is, both on account of its popularity and the sense of superiority in it, to say nothing of its singularity, by which alone it has a good right to be a metropolis, for as a kingdom can have but one metropolis, and in all the king's dominions there is but one Greenock, it follows of course that it is *de facto* a metropolis. . ."[16]

Galt wrote that he had been cruelly disappointed in the town's prospects when he discovered that estimates "in which I had been led to expect a considerable business might be formed, (were) in a great measure fallacious."[17] In *The Steamboat* (1822), Galt's narrator, a Glasgow merchant, chides the residents of Greenock for their "great notions" about their town's culture and prosperity, "for a town like Greenock is overly near to our great city ever to have a genteel independency in its own community to maintain such establishments with a suitable bravery."[18]

Galt's conception of cities was basically formed by the contrasting characters of Glasgow and Edinburgh. He was usually impressed with Glasgow's commercial vitality but also hinted at the excessive self-interest of "this profit and loss city."[19] His narrator in *The Entail* describes the trend in which "the general merchants of the royal city began to arrogate to themselves that aristocratic superiority over the shopkeepers which they have since established into an oligarchy as proud and sacred. . . as the famous seigniories of Venice and Genoa."[20] Galt never seemed comfortable, on the other hand, in Edinburgh, even though many of his publishing and literary connections were there. He usually refers to it sarcastically as "the intellectual city" and "the Athens of the North," and a favorite topic of many of his fictional travellers was the mediocrity of its intellectual establishment which was "so little known out of the circles of the intellectual city, while they are so strenuously celebrated within its bounds."[21]

Some of the finest descriptions of nineteenth century Scottish urban form appear in Galt's works. Glasgow's streets were characterized as "spreading as if they were one of the branches of cotton-spinning,"[22] and he pokes some fun at "the stately houses and plantations that our principal merchants and manufacturers have built on high and pleasant places, thicker and thicker, till they are lost in the smoke and confusion of our Tarshish."[23] One of Galt's visitors to Edinburgh felt that the "rugged, veteran aspect of the Old Town is agreeably contrasted with the bright, smooth forehead of the New."[24] But Galt usually had his characters react negatively to "the forlorn silence of the new town"[25] and the rigidity of its plan, with its "houses grown up as if they were sown in the seed-time with the corn by a drill machine, or dibbled in rigs and furrows like beans and potatoes."[26] But if these cities fell short of some urban ideal, Galt nevetheless regarded them as prototypes of urban excellence compared to some of the cities of the ancient world. The traveller in "The Jaunt" is only half-jesting when he objects to Edinburgh being referred to as the "Athens of the North" by its academics because Athens as a city was not worthy of emulation; "its well kenn'd that men who get their wits from books are not very accurate in their knowledge, or they would never go to compare the town of Edinburgh with such a heap of mason-shivers as Athens is."[27]

Galt had a lifelong fascination with London as a great metropolis. Its immensity made a strong impression on him when he first saw it in 1804, as in this letter to his cousin Jeannie back in Irvine:

Its size is beyond the mind of an individual to comprehend which renders it beyond description. In some parts it exalts my expectation, the effect of the whole however is not remarkable. In my opinion its dimensions are its greatest magnificence and these seem almost to partake of the infinite as they reach on every side beyond the power of the eye.[28]

His first impression was repeated in several literary works, but probably most effectively in *The Ayrshire Legatees,* after a residence in London of several years.

Vast masses of dark, low-hung clouds were mingled with the smokey canopy; and the dome of St. Paul's, like the enormous idol of some terrible deity, throned amidst the smoke of sacrifices and magnificance, darkness and mystery, presented altogether an object of vast sublimity. . . and unceasing sound, like the enginery of an earthquake at work, rolls from the heart of that profound and indefinable obscurity; sometimes a faint and yellow beam of sun strikes here and there in the vast expanse of edifices, and churches and holy asylums are dimly seen lifting up their countless steeples and spires — like so many lightning rods to avert the wrath of Heaven.[29]

Unlike William Cobbett's trenchant social observations on London at about the same time, Galt's comments tend to ignore the growing problem of the urban poor or the fear of social disorder. Galt's observers admit that "the crowd that fills the streets is more friendless than the sands of the Arabian desert, or the trees of the American woods,"[30] and occasionally his characters try to capture the subtle quality of the metropolitan way of life, as in the conclusion that "the absence of delicacy. . . is characteristic of all the varieties of the metropolitan mind."[31] But most of Galt's evaluations of London are positive and Scottish cities tend to be compared unfavorably. Edinburgh's elite, for example, was similar to that of London's, "but the flavour of the metropolitan style is wanting."[32] And the Glaswegian traveller in *The Steamboat* was impressed with the "natural instinct of civilization" which characterized pedestrian traffic in London compared with the rustic "dinging, and bumping, and driving that happens in the Trongate, especially. . . when the farmers and their kintra wives" were in the city on market day.[33]

Galt's urban consciousness also extended to the question of how towns can be effective agencies of social policy and territorial expansion. In commenting on the over abundance of the British rural population in 1822 he suggested that "the policy which induced the great statesmen of antiquity to build and settle cities, is a branch of political economy that has not received the attention it deserves."[34] His proposed solution represented a strong Scottish tradition: "far better it were to devise some means of concentrating into new towns those whom so many theorists have rendered restless, than to squander the public stock on them in settlements in distant islands."[35] It is not clear how well informed Galt was about the new town movement in Scotland and Ireland. Between 1700 and 1850, more than six hundred towns and villages were planted, most of them by large landowners who had already done or were doing what Galt was recommending.[36] In *The Ayrshire Legatees* he does mention the new town of Ardrossan, founded in 1805 by an aristocrat as a canal-head seaport. One of his characters exclaims: "What a monument has the late Earl of Eglinton left there of his public spirit! It should embalm his memory in the hearts of future ages, as I doubt not but in time Ardrossan will become a grand emporium."[37]

Colonial settlements had interested Galt as early as 1807, some twenty years before he actually founded a town. After conversations with a cousin and schoolmate from Irvine, William Gilkinson, who had spent about a decade as a ship's captain in the Great Lakes, Galt put forward a general evaluation of those who had launched settlement ventures.

> There are no historical facts more valuable than those which relate to the formation of communities, and the origin of nations; nor perhaps, are the narratives of conquerers more interesting than the plain tales of those who, by the virtue of their design alone, have improved the condition of mankind.[38]

William Penn was held up as a noble example as was the Earl of Selkirk, for his settlement in Upper Canada, where he had "built a village for the Highlanders, and they are now very comfortably established."[39]

By 1824, when he was deeply involved in the organization of a Canadian colonization scheme, his ideas were more fully developed. He strongly advocated the notion of "directed settlement," for two much emigration "has been conducted on erroneous principles. Poor families have been transplanted, with their poverty, into wild regions, and left in a manner there to shift for themselves."[40] But this direction should not come from government, as was the case with Wilmot Horton's project of transporting Irish paupers to Upper Canada under the superintendence of Peter Robinson. Rather, Galt believed, the impetus should come from commercial interests. In rhetorical fashion he asked: would not Upper Canadian settlement have been more successful if it "had been under the auspices of some opulent commercial company — habitations and subsistence provided for them — their labour judiciously directed, and aided with the help of machinery?"[41]

After his first visit to North American in 1825, Galt's practical knowledge of the settlement process was greatly enhanced. He now referred to the Australian and Van Dieman's Land companies in favorable terms but saved his highest accolades for the "American speculators" whose method of settlement had been "reduced into a system."[42] On his way to Upper Canada in 1825 as a commissioner appointed to help evaluate the price of land, Galt had visited two land companies that had developed much of central and western New York state. Galt learned that Charles Williamson, as head of the Pulteny holdings, had pioneered the concept of providing cleared land, roads, houses and fairly complete towns, but Galt recognized that "an injudicious prodigality of expenditure" had very nearly scuttled the whole operation.[43] The Holland Land Company, on the other hand, which developed a large tract and founded towns such as Batavia and Buffalo, usually provided only the rudiments of a village and access roads to other established communities. In a report back to the Directors of the Canada Company he emphasized the successes of the two companies: the founding of 212 towns and villages, a population of about half a million and an extensive amount of manufacturing."[44]

The system, as he described it in *Blackwood's Magazine,* was relatively simple.

> They begin in some convenient situation, chosen for hydraulic purposes, by erecting a tavern for the accommodation of settlers, until they can construct houses for themselves — a mill and a smithy are the next objects; then a store is opened, and subsequently a temporary church and school-house. These constitute the original elements, the nucleus of an American city.[45]

Galt visited the American projects again in late 1826 on his way to Upper Canada on a "special mission of inquiry and investigation" for the Canada Company, a position which evolved into that of superintendent of operations. The American companies opened their books for his examination and he resolved to adopt their administrative practices as well as their policies on the nature of credit and repayment and gifts of land to churches.[46] Galt later wrote that he had passed through the country west of Utica no less than nine times. Not surprisingly, the system of settlement devised there was to become the most direct model for his subsequent Canadian enterprises.

The novel *Lawrie Todd* (1830) was based on his knowledge of New York's development, and provides a useful primer on the reasons for frontier town growth or failure. Even more revealing were his "Letters from New York," published in 1829 and 1830.[47] They effectively contrast the North American wilderness with the suddenly created instant towns. The forest itself was not the friendly European version and it filled him with a sense of awe and mystery.

> The interior of the woods is singularly silent — I would say, is awful. When the air is calm, scarcely a sound of any kind is to be heard, for the few birds that flit athwart the gloom are dumb. It is impossible that the European emigrant can enter such solitudes to form his habitation, without dread; nor the traveller to contemplate his condition without participation in his anxieties and fears.[48]

The metaphors Galt uses in describing the settlement process in New York state are similar to those which American town boosters were using on other American frontiers, but Galt's imagery is based on a more cosmopolitan experience.[49] An example:

When you have seen. . . the style of the forest, the moors of Scotland are more interesting as far as the landscape is concerned. To the political economist, however, no portion of the world presents scenes so interesting. The towns rise like mushrooms. I never see a steeple peering over the woods, without thinking of the growth of Jack's bean-stalk.[50]

Or, on the new quality of the new towns:

From Utica westward, the age of the different towns is an object of curiosity. In Europe, the antiquity of a place is supposed to be in some way associated with honour, but the American towns are like ladies out of their teens, they wish to be considered as juvenile as may be.[51]

The Canadian Experiment

Galt's arrival in Upper Canada late in 1826 marked the end of a long and complicated process whereby the largest and most powerful commercial organization in Upper Canada was created.[52] It also marked the beginning of a tangled tale of conflicts, intrigues, misunderstandings and questionable judgement as a great colonization venture began its operations. The origins of the Canada Company grew almost accidentally out of Galt's efforts on behalf of Upper Canadians claiming war losses; these negotiations involved the highest levels of the British government including Lord Liverpool, the Prime Minister; Lord Bathurst, the Secretary of State for the colonies; and Wilmot Horton, the colonial undersecretary. When British officials made it clear they could not raise the necessary funds, Galt suggested the sale of the crown and clergy reserves of land in Upper Canada, and discussions continued on that basis.[53] By 1824 Galt was instrumental in forming a joint stock company, based on investors who made up the financial aristocracy of London, who, not incidentally, seemed to deal of confidence in Galt's business acumen. His role as author was played down in these circumstances. For example, when sending a completed manuscript to one of his publishers he asked that his name not be used: "You know my parliamentary concerns and some folks are apt to think business may be neglected."[54]

Getting a parliamentary charter for the company would require another two years of compicated and frustrating bargaining. During this time Galt was dismayed to learn from Bathurst that the monies to be raised from the land sales were not going to be used to compensate the war claimants.[55] He also slowly became aware of the prickly character of the small oligarchy which dominated the political, economic and social life of the province. The leading figure of the group, Rev. John Strachan, successfully lobbied in London against the sale of the clergy reserves to the company. A compromise solution substituted a million acre tract in the Lake Huron area for the clergy reserves. The charter, finalized in August, 1826, included the sale of the Huron tract, the 42,000 acre Halton Block near York (Toronto) and more than a million acres of crown reserves scattered throughout the province. The price was an average of 3s 6d per acre, or a total of £344,375 2d, payable over sixteen years. An important rider from Galt's point of view as a colonizer was that one-third of the purchase price of the tract and block could be spent by the company on public improvements.[56]

In several respects the colonizing venture was launched under the worst possible circumstances. Provincial officials such as Lieutenant-Governor Peregrine Maitland and John Strachan were extremely jealous and suspicious of the introduction of any new, competing authority into their tidy, but increasingly tense domain. When Galt arrived he must have been nonplussed by a waiting letter from Strachan warning him "to support the Colonial authorities and never take a side against them" and advising him that "you will frequently require the assistance of me and my friends. But in order to receive that assistance, indeed in order to enable us to give it, you must confide in us and in us alone."[57] The Canada Company itself was by no means a well organized or monolithic entity. Not only were lines of authority not clearly drawn in terms of decision-making, but the loss of the clergy reserves had changed much of the basis of the early organization and investment, and many shareholders were understandably skeptical about the new format. As a result, the Directors were much more likely to insist on instant results and profits than originally envisaged.

It says a good deal about Galt's personality that he sailed ahead, seemingly oblivious to the troubled waters surrounding him. He apparently decided very quickly not to make the town of York his headquarters, ridiculing its metropolitan pretensions. He later wrote that "every body who has ever been at Dover knows that it is one of the vilest blue-devil haunts on the face of the earth, except Little York in U. Canada, when he has been there one day."[58] Instead, early in 1827 he sent a surveyor, George Tiffany, to examine the Halton block and report on the possibility of founding a central, company town. Tiffany was impressed with the quality of the soil and made special mention of a "rise of Ground where there is a beautiful site for a Town." He also commented on the water power potential of the site and believed it would not be difficult to build a road from it to the existing road to Waterloo county which had been settled by Pennsylvania Mennonites.[59] Galt lost no time in accepting Tiffany's report and recommended the site as the location of the company's office to the Directors.[60] To ensure the suitability of the choice, however, he directed the company's recently hired "Warden of the Forest," Dr. William "Tiger" Dunlop, an old Scottish Friend, to return to the block with Tiffany and another surveyor, John McDonald. By this time, March 19th, 1827, Galt was referring to "the proposed site of the City of Guelph."[61] Dunlop and his crew began their examination on April 4th and concurrred in Tiffany's previous report.[62]

At this stage of the operation, Galt did not feel it necessary to get approval from the London office before initiating the first of several possible towns, probably because the system of planting towns in order to stimulate settlement had been considered the acceptable practice by company officials ever since Galt's first trip to New York State. Thus, while he asked the Directors for "enlarged credit" for "carrying into effect the preparation" — they allowed him £4,000 — he planned to "proceed with the necessary works. I have given orders for the construction of certain log-houses or shanties for the reception of Tradesmen and Settlers, for the Ground to be cleared, the Road to be laid open, and a Building for a Tavern to be erected." He also suggested selling town lots at $20 each and putting half of the income toward the building of a school. "This principle," he believed, "with respect to Towns and Villages will reflect honor on the Company. . ."[63]

Galt also gave some thought to the kind of immigrant the company might expect. He later wrote that he "imagined upon theoretic principles, that to give employment to pauper emigrants ought to be the first step, before a better class could be allured to come."[64] The better class he and the company had in mind, of course, was made up of those who would have the necessary money to buy farms or to set up commercial and industrial activities in the towns. But the life-long Tory also dreamed of attracting aristocrats to the Company's lands — while he admired American commercial dynamism he did not appreciate the political and social implications of the age of the common man. Writing to Wilmot Horton in February and April, 1827, he claimed that the present Canadian land system "is only calculated to breed democrats." In terms reminiscent of Upper Canada's first Lieutenant-Governor, John Graves Simcoe, Galt argued that if an aristocracy were to be established, it would be possible to "encourage the younger members of the Aristocratic families, who do not choose to adopt professions, to become the Leaders of Settlers." He personally knew of five or six "with no Americanism about them."[65]

The ceremonial beginnings of the company's operations revealed Galt's sense of occasion and his undoubted gifts as a promoter. The formal founding of Guelph was set for April 23rd. Galt and the group of surveyors who had chosen the spot for Guelph assembled in the closest village to the company's block, a place appropriately renamed Galt in Galt's honour by his friend William Dickson. The Scottish relationship between these two men is not clear, but Dickson was one of the major war losses claimants. Significantly, Dickson had done on a minor scale what Galt was about to do at Guelph. He had purchased a block of about 94,000 acres in 1816, which he named Dumfries Township, and with his manager, Absalom Shade, had erected mills, a store, and other facilities "to render the tract valuable."[66] The village of Galt, as that of its younger cousin, Guelph, was oriented, in terms of metropolitan connections, not to York (Toronto) but to Burlington Bay at the western point of Lake Ontario with its three small villages — Dundas, Ancaster and Hamilton.[67]

On the morning of April 23, the group walked the eighteen miles from the village of Galt to the proposed site, arriving after sunset. According to Galt

> It was consistent with my plan to invest our ceremony with a little mystery, the better to make it remembered. So intimating that the main body of men were not to come, we walked to the brow of the neighbouring rising ground, and Mr. Prior having shewn the site selected for the town, a large maple tree was chosen; on which, taking an axe from one of the woodsmen, I struck the first stroke. To me at least the moment was impressive, — and the silence of the woods, that echoed to the sound, was as the sigh of the solemn genius of the wilderness departing for ever.

After "the tree fell with a crash of accumulating thunder. . . there was a funereal pause. . . of short duration, for the doctor pulled a flask of whiskey from his bosom, and we drank prosperity to the City of Guelph."[68]

The date of the founding, St. George's Day, seems to have been one aspect of Galt's promotional effort. In his *Autobiography,* he wrote that the date

> was not without design; I was well aware of the boding effect of a little solemnity of the minds of most men, and especially of the unlettered, such as the first class of settlers were likely to be, at eras which betokened destiny, like the launching of a vessel, or the birth of an enterprise, of which a horoscope might be cast. The founding of a town was certainly one of these.[69]

Galt also referred to the conscious choice of the date in several private letters.[70] To the Directors of the Company, however, his portrayal of the event was more in keeping with what might be regarded as strictly business, for "By an agreeable and unforseen circumstance the first Tree was felled on St. George's Day."[71]

A second promotional device was the name of the new town. He personally chose Guelph "in compliment to the royal family, both because I thought it auspicious in itself, and because I could not recollect that it had ever been before used in all the King's dominions."[72] The royal family, the Hanoverians, were descended from the Guelphs, one of the great political factions in late medieval Germany and Italy. Galt's choice was probably based on a desire for publicity and prestige, for he had no great respect for the Hanoverians as a dynasty. For example, in a children's history textbook he had earlier claimed that "no usurpation was ever achieved with greater treachery, nor pursued with more cruelty of spirit, than the Hanoverian acquisition of the British crown."[73] The Directors in London believed it was a mistake to use such an important name for a town in the relatively small Halton Block and suggested Galt reserve it for a future town in the much larger Huron Tract.[74] Galt refused to use the name they substituted — Goderich — but did apply it to the second town, a port on Lake Huron, later that same year.[75]

A third promotional device was the imaginative town plan Galt devised for the site. This represented a significant departure from the monotonous grid which typified most planted towns in British North America, for it involved the use of a concept of streets radiating from a focal point in Renaissance ideal town fashion. The conception and implementation of the plan took several weeks. According to the surveyor, George Tiffany, he

> had personal conferences with Mr. Galt as to the laying out of the town. [I then] drew a plan or sketch which did not altogether meet Mr. Galt's approbation, and then, after receiving instructions from Mr. Galt, drew a map, which was approved of, and in accordance with which the town was laid out.[76]

On April 30th Galt wrote the Directors that "the plan. . . will be finished next week" and then lots and millseats could be selected by those who had determined to buy them.[77] Laying out the site took longer than expected. By June 14th he was vexed to report that the survey was still incomplete.

> The minuteness requisite to a Town Plan, and the great deficiency of science with respect to levelling among the Surveyors has given me both much vexation and trouble, for although I made a point to employ the best talent attainable on every occasion, the best is but mediocre. The enclosed sketch affords some idea of the scheme on which the Town is projected, but the clearing of the Wood is constantly inducing alterations from the undulating character of the ground.[78]

While neither the sketch to which Galt refers, nor Tiffany's original plan have been found, we do have a copy of Tiffany's plan drawn by surveyor John McDonald in 1828.[79] The published lithograph is based on either Tiffany's or McDonald's plans and is a generally accurate depiction of Galt's design.[80] Several features of this plan are noteworthy. First, the radial street pattern focussed in symmetrical fashion on the ceremonial maple tree stump in what was known as Priory Place. This made possible a dramatic terminating vista in Renaissance style, but the fan-shaped pattern also was a sensible solution to the problem of developing the peninsular site bounded by the Speed River. Second, the triangular "market ground" represented a large amount of public space, acting as the focal point for early commercial and social activity. Third, symbolically important sites were granted to several churches. The Catholics received "a beautiful central hill" as a reward for Bishop Macdonell's support, and the Episcopalians were granted St. George's Square, in what seems to have been an effort to placate Archdeacon Strachan. "Another rising ground" was reserved for the Presbyterians but it is unclear if this was meant to be the site they eventually purchased in the market ground.[81] Fourth, the awkward connection between the radiating pattern and the grid organization of the rest of the site led to some very difficult corners and unusual block shapes. It also reveals that Galt's imagination as a town planner was not matched by experience, especialy when dealing with a rough, wilderness site.

Like the Guelph plan, the Goderich plan which followed later that same year also had a dramatic flair but was a more successful merging of radial and grid patterns. (Plan No. 4) It too was designed by Galt. The question is, what town planning traditions are represented by these plans? One obvious source was Scotland — the new trend in Edinburgh planning which emerged during the competition for an extension of the New Town north of Calton Hill. Between 1813 and the 1820s the city corporation directed a reaction against the eighteenth century Georgian design of James Craig with its two squares set in a grid. It accepted the proposal of William Playfair whose plan involved several streets diverging from a central point, a principle he believed had long been shown to be effective "particularly in the Piazza del Popola at Rome." [82] Very little of Playfair's design was ever implemented but Galt was often in the city when the plans were the subject of intense local interest.[83]

The other major source for Galt was the tradition represented by Washington, D.C. or at least by some of its mid-American offspring. The immediate example may have been Buffalo, built by the Holland Land Company as the site for its land office. Its planner, Joseph Ellicott, was a brother of Andrew Ellicott who had replaced L'Enfant as the planner of Washington. Galt regarded Buffalo, with its radiating street pattern, as a "very prosperous and handsome town."[84] Buffalo was not an isolated example on the American frontier for designs of this type were used in many other places including Detroit. Galt's design for Goderich somewhat resembles that of Alexander Ralston's 1821 plan of Indianapolis — Ralston had been a surveyor in Washington — but there is no evidence of any direct connection with Galt.[85] (Plan Nos. 5 and 6) In terms of planning as a promotional tool, Galt's efforts should probably be judged a success. For example, when Joseph Bouchette published six town plans in his *The British Dominions in North America* (1831) he included Guelph and Goderich, not because these towns warranted that sort of status but because of their unusual (by Canadian standards) plans.

For the actual building of the town of Guelph, Galt hired as superintendent of operations a young Englishman with surveying and farming experience, Charles Prior. Perhaps more than any other company official, Prior was infected with Galt's dream of Guelph's future greatness. Three major projects represented the company's contribution to town building during the first year. One was road building, with roads northeast to Eramosa township and another northwest to Woolwich-Nichol township. The most ambitious road project was that of the Waterloo Road, seven miles in length, and exceptionally wide (130 feet of clearing). In terms that would rival those of any town booster anywhere, Galt proudly described the road as "the glory of Guelph. . . an avenue, with trees on each side far exceeding in height the most stupendous in England. . . the high road to the town lay along the middle of this Babylonian approach."[86]

A second large project was clearing of part of the generously-sized townsite. By mid-May Prior was employing one hundred men in "Chopping, Burning, Levelling Ground, Cutting House Logs. . . quarrying stone, burning lime, cutting the Road from Waterloo" and so on. According to Prior they were "men of all Countries, Irish, Scotch, Americans, Dutch, Germans, Indian and Negroes, all strangers to the place and to each other, having only one object in common, to obtain as much money and to do as little for it as possible."[87] Visitors were amazed at the large-scale activity of felling and burning of trees. One wrote his wife in June about the giant trees "crumbling into ashes or blazing into flames. I thought more of the smoking ruins of Moscow than of the rising importance of Guelph."[88] By the summer some of the central area had been cleared. After this the company left lots to be cleared by those purchasing them, concentrating instead on opening the major streets.

A third area of company activity was the construction of several public buildings. The centrepiece was the Priory, a large log house or caravansary jokingly named after Prior. The original function of this house was to accommodate settlers while their houses in town or in the town's vicinity were being built. Occasionally it held almost one hundred persons at a time; in 1828 it was converted to a residence for Galt and his family. Other public buildings were a market house, a school — built with funds from one-half of the sale price of some early lots — and the company assisted with the construction of a tavern.

Galt was understandably enthusiastic about the "new city. . . which is progressing beyond all expectations."[89] Visitors were flocking to see the project, he wrote the Directors, "for the proceedings begin to make some noise in the Country."[90] By October 1st about seventy houses were built, the company having assisted early settlers in this regard, a policy that "was absolutely necessary to form a nucleus round which the future Town might grow" Prior reported.[91] Town and farm lots were apparently selling briskly, with prices for town lots ranging from $20 to $40 and farm land from $1.50 to $2.50 an acre. The downpayment on agricultural land was one-fifth of the total and was often paid for by labour on the roads or townsite. As the settlement at and near Guelph was developing rapidly, the exploration and surveying of the huge Huron tract to the west was also moving ahead.

The perceptions of these developments depended, however, on the viewer's location. From Guelph, Galt wrote his cousin in Irvine that he was "the second person in this great country with a lordly income and a power which in its administration already affects the happiness of thousands and will probably influence the destiny of their descendants for ages to come."[92] He was well aware of the fact that his views and those of the Directors differed considerably. In June, 1827, he wrote a friend that "I fear the gentry in St. Helen's place are too impatient for returns. They expect the ship to be earning a freight before she is launched."[93] To the Directors meeting at their office at 13 St. Helen's Place, just off Bishopsgate in London, the clear and only purpose of the land company's enterprise was profit on their investment. They seemed caught between a clamouring group of shareholders on the one hand, and on the other by a superintendent in Canada who seemed determined to make major decisions without their prior approval and who reported his accounts only in the most vague and informal manner.

The first bone of contention between Galt and the Directors involved the question of strategic decisions such as the founding of Guelph which Galt had made on his own. Later in 1827 the Directors ruled that "It will be for the Court (of Directors) to decide whether the selection of the site as well as the details of location ought in all cases to be left to the discretion of the Superintendent" and Galt was forced, in a somewhat chastised manner, to put forward plans for Goderich as a proposal rather than as an accomplished fact.[94] An equally serious area of conflict was the manner in which Galt reported expenditures and land sales to the London authorities. Officials eventually sent out an accountant, Thomas Smith, in 1828, whose relationship with Galt quickly deteriorated, especially after Smith's highly critical but questionable reports back to London. A measure of the Directors' loss of confidence in Galt is the tone of a letter to him in November, 1828, in which they suggest he review his correspondence of the last twelve months "and consider how much of it is occupied by personal discussions of no utility to the affairs of the company."[95] Other issues also complicated the relationship, including Galt's charitable action towards a group of refugees known as the La Guayran settlers, and rumours about tensions between him and the provincial oligarchy. The growing rift between Galt and the company became unbridgeable. On his way back to England early in 1829 to explain his case, Galt learned of his recall in an item in a Montreal newspaper.

The new order of things became apparent in Guelph almost immediately. Even before the new superintendent, Thomas Mercer Jones, arrived, an overlay on the official plan, dated April 8, 1829, greatly reduced the amount of public space at Priory Place and effectively destroyed the symmetrical character of the focal point; some of the streets now joined it rather awkwardly. (Plan No. 2) As well, company officials attempted to claim the market ground as company land by pencilling in dotted lines and on later maps by strengthening these to heavy lines. They also greatly reduced the amount of land Galt had granted to the Catholic church.[96]

Ironically, the company took pride in what Galt's system had accomplished and used it in its advertisements to encourage immigrants, as on this broadsheet of 1833:

> In the short space of five years, a town has been established in the wilderness with churches, schools, stores, taverns, and mills; and where there are mechanics of every kind, and a society has been formed of a highly respectable description. Property has improved in value at from 250 to 1000 per cent, thus showing beyond the possibility of doubt, the advantages which the plan adopted by the Canada Company in the settlement of their lands have conferred upon the Emigrant. The same plans being adhered to in the Huron Tract, there is every reason to expect similar results.[97]

Galt could not have said it better himself, for the advertisement seemed to recognise the principle that the company's operations were more than purely a commercial venture. But the limited and one-sided approach that had been expected of him while in Canada had led to the creation of a sequel of sorts to his Canada Company experience. In 1828 Galt put forward a proposal for a new colony in Lower Canada — with himself as part of "its chief management" — to Lord Dalhousie, Governor General resident in Quebec City.[98] While his current Canada Company position gave him "an ample opportunity of gratifying my inclination for colonizing, "the problem was that the role of colonizer was "a task of more various cares than should rest on the shoulders of a mere mercantile agent."[99] Nothing came of his specific proposal, but after his return to Britain he managed to organize another commercial venture much along the lines of the Canada Company, called the British American Land Company, and centered at Sherbrooke in the Eastern Townships of Lower Canada. Ill health prevented him from taking up an administrative position, but his son Alex rose to the position of Commissioner with the new company.[100]

In what could be termed a decade of reflection after his Canadian experience, Galt put considerable effort into justifying his "experiment." Much of his *Autobiography* was devoted to that end, and included detailed financial statements and reprints of letters to relevant officials. The extent to which his town founding schemes were involved in his difficulties with the Directors was ruefully acknowledged.

> But Guelph. . . was like all cities fated with a high destiny, the cause of quarrels. . . for from the day that I announced the birth of this metropolis to the Diectors of the Canada Company, my troubles and vexations began.[101]

Two works of fiction written soon after his return from Canada allowed him to reassert some of the principles he had followed in promoting a particular kind of settlement process. In *Lawrie Todd* (1830), the setting was the new towns and the frontier of upstate New York; according to Galt, the history of Judiville in the book was "a shadowy and subdued outline of the history and localities of Rochester."[102] The central theme was "the rise and progress of a successful American settlement," with an emphasis on speculation, commerce and economic growth. More closely connected to his own colonization efforts was *Bogle Corbet* (1831) which featured a colonizer founding "Stockwell" with the felling of a tree on a site encompassed on three sides by the river "Slant." Included here was one of Galt's clearest statements of his policy, buttressed by logic, experience and history.

> Reflection on the effect and situation of towns in the old country, as well as the best information to be obtained respecting the system adopted by the Americans in settling their wild lands, has persuaded me, that the first effectual step in colonization is to plant a village. . . Indeed the plan is so obviously judicious, that two opinions cannot be entertained on the subject; for we see it is from towns in all countries that cultivation proceeds; and history, in describing the colonies of antiquity, distinctly shows that the first object was ever the choice of a proper site for a fortress or a city.[103]

Bogle Corbet cuts to the heart of Galt's thinking about the nature of community. On the one hand he was attracted by the commercial dynamism of the American approach which featured the kind of frontier individualism Frederick Jackson Turner would later extoll as the chief characteristic of Americanism. And the Canada Company represented the transition from imperial government sponsored and directed settlement projects to those with a commercial base. But Galt believed that his self-interest, and by extension, the interest of the company whose colonizing venture he managed, should be balanced by responsibility to the community that was created.[104] In practise, this involved a strong dose of paternalism. The colonizer in *Bogle Corbet* provided strong leadership through a company store, by serving as a magistrate and by setting up a system of law enforcement. Galt had concerned himself personally with activities of that sort and had tried to stimulate a sense of community by organizing festivities and fairs. He continued to refer warmly to "my city" long after his removal from Canada. This utopian element in his approach combined the functions of civilization and control. Its proprietary aspects had been well developed in earlier phases of town building and colonization under the direction of imperial officials.[105] It was to be become part of a local Upper Canadian tradition, partially inspired by Galt, with the founding of the village of Elora by his cousin, William Gilkison, in 1832; and the founding of Fergus by Adam Fergusson in 1833.[106] It represented the major distinguishing feature of Canadian towns when compared to those in the United States.[107] In this respect the rich record Galt left of his activities and thoughts provides a unique insight into a significant phase of early Canadian development.

NOTES

[1]To David Moir, October 5, 1828, Galt Papers, Public Archieves of Canada. (PAC)

[2]The most successful effort to study both sides of Galt is H.B. Timothy, *The Galts: A Canadian Odyssey, John Galt 1779- 1839* (Toronto: McClelland and Stewart, 1977). The standard work on his fiction is Ian Gordon, *John Galt, The Life of A Writer* (London: Oliver and Boyd, 1972). Gordon's work is also extremely important in determining the authorship of many of Galt's unsigned essays. Among the most useful studies of his North American experience are Elizabeth Waterston, "John Galt, the Founder of Guelph," *Historic Guelph,* vol. 17 (1977-78), 4-15, and Clarence Karr, "The Two Sides of John Galt," *Ontario History,* vol. 59 (1967), 93-100.

[3]Galt to J.G. Lockhart, July 4, 1836, Letters to Lockhart, MS. 925, National Library of Scotland.

[4]*The Literary Life and Miscellanies of John Galt* (Edinburgh: William Blackwood, 1834), vol. 1, 354.

[5]Lockhart to Galt, August 31, 1830, MS 10998, National Library of Scotland.

[6]He had published *The Battle of Largs* (1804). My appreciation of Galt's literary status does not extend to his poetry (at least not yet).

[7]See, for example, Anand C. Chitnis, "The Scottish Enlightenment in the Age of Galt," in Christopher A. Whatley, ed., *John Galt 1779-1979* (Edinburgh: Ramsay Head Press, 1979), 31-50, and Keith M. Costain, "The Prince and the Provost," *Studies in Scottish Literature,* vol. 6 (June, 1968), 20-35.

[8]Adam Smith, *The Wealth of Nations* (New York: Modern Library, 1937), 392, in Bk. 3, chp. 4, entitled "How the Commerce of the Towns contributed to the improvement of the Country."

[9]For some of the excellent literature available on this theme see Raymond Williams, *The Country and the City* (London: Chatto & Windus, 1973); Carl Schorske, "The Idea of the City in European Thought: Voltaire to Spengler," in Oscar Handlin and John Burchard, eds., *The Historian and the City* (Cambridge, Mass., M.I.T. Press, 1963), 95-114; Andrew Lees, "Perceptions of Cities in Britain and Germany, 1820-1914," in Derek Fraser and Anthony Sutcliffe, eds., *The Pursuit of Urban History* (London: Edward Arnold, 1983), 151-166.

[10]*Literary Life,* I, 226.

[11]*Annals of the Parish* (Edinburgh: John Grant, 1936), I, 183.

[12]*Ibid.,* II, 32

[13]*Ibid.,* I, 177.

[14]*Literary Life,* I, 219

[15]*Lawrie Todd,* or, *The settlers in the woods* London: Scott, Colburn and Bentley 1832), 258.

[16]From "The man of genius," a four page fragment of a story in Galt's handwriting, on paper watermarked 1836; probably unpublished. Goodwin-Haines Collection, University of Guelph Archives (UGA).

[17]*Literary Life,* I, 221.

[18]*The steam-boat* (Edinburgh: William Blackwood, 1822), 125-6.

[19]*Glenfell, or Macdonalds and Campbells. An Edinburgh tale of the nineteenth century* (London: Richard Phillips, 1820), 225.

[20](Edinburgh: John Grant, 1936). 202.

[21]*Glenfell,* 161. Among many similar examples is *The Majolo: a tale* (London: I. Faulkner, 1816), vol. 2, 97, 105.

[22]*The Ayrshire Legatees* (Edinburgh: John Grant, 1936), 81.

[23]*Steamboat,* 101.

[24]*Ayrshire Legatees,* 87.

[25]*Glenfell,* 53.

[26]*Ayrshire Legatees,* 81.

[27]In *Stories of the study,* vol. 3 (London: Cochrane and McCrone, 1833), 82-3. Galt's negative impression of Athens and other ancient cities is clearly spelled out in his accounts of his travels; *Voyages and travels, in the years 1809-1810, and 1811* (London: Cadell and Davis, 1812), 184; and *Letters from the Levant* (London: Cadell and Davis, 1813), 113.

[28]Galt to Jeannie Spirling, July 4, 1805, Galt Correspondence, Lizars Collection, UGA.

[29]*Ayrshire Legatees,* 86. Also, *Majolo,* vol. 2, 47- 8.

[30]*Bogle Corbet, or, the emigrants* (London: Colburn and Bentley, 1831), vol. I, 118.

[31]*Ayrshire Legatees,* 200.

[32]*Ibid.,* 120.

[33]*Steamboat,* 173-4.

[34]"Hints to the country gentleman, I," *Blackwood's Magazine,* vol. 12 (October, 1822, 488.

[35]*Ibid.,* 489.

[36]D.G. Lockhart, "Planned village development in Scotland and Ireland, 1700-1850," in T.M. Devine and David Dickson, eds., *Ireland and Scotland, 1600-1850; Parellels and contrasts in economic and social development* (Edinburgh: Donald, 1983); 132-45; and Colin McWilliams, *Scottish townscape* (London: Collins, 1975, chp. V.

[37]75.

[38]"A statistical account of Upper Canada," *The Philosophical Magazine,* vol. 29 (October, 1807), 7.

[39]*Ibid. 8.*

[40]"Bandana on emigration. Letter first," *Blackwood's Magazine,* vol. 15 (April, 1824), 434.

[41]*Ibid.*

[42]*"Bandana on colonial undertakings," Blackwood's magazine,* vol. 20 (August, 1826), 305. For a good outline of Galt's involvement with the New York land companies, see Clarence Karr, *The Canada land company: the early years, an experiment in colonization, 1823-1843* (Ottawa: Ontario Historical Society, 1974), chps. I and II.

[43]"Bandana on colonial undertakings," 305.

[44]"Summary relative to the land speculations by which the Genesee Country and the Western Territory of New York were settled," Canada Company Papers (CCP), Public Archives of Ontario (PAO).

[45]"Bandana on colonial undertakings," 305.

[46]Galt to Court of Directors, Nov. 23, Dec. 16, Dec. 28, 1826. CCP, PAO.

[47]These letters were simply signed "A", but are clearly Galt's work. For the Galt authorship, see Linda Jones, "John Galt: An addition to his Bibliography," *Studies in Scottish literature,* vol. 9 (July, 1971), 55-58.

[48]"Letters from New York, V," *New Monthly Magazine,* vol. 28 (1830), 239.

[49]See for example the efforts of Dr. Daniel Drake as described by Richard Wade, *The urban frontier* (Chicago: University of Chicago Press, 1959) 156-157.

[50]"Letters from New York, V," 241.

[51]*Ibid.,* IV (1830), 55.

[52]The most detailed and accurate account of the formation of the company is Roger Hall, "The Canada Company, 1826-1843," (Unpublished Ph.D. dissertation, University of Cambridge, 1973). Galt, unfortunately, is usually referred to as "the novelist" and therefore an outsider in the business world; his actions tend to be judged only from the perspective of the profit ledger.

[53]This suggestion was first made to him by his friend Bishop Alexander Macdonell. Galt later wrote that it was "from this circumstance the Canada Company was ultimately formed." *The autobiography of John Galt,* London: Cochrane and McCrone, 1833), vol. I, pp. 294-5.

[54]To Oliver and Boyd, Dec. 4, 1823, Oliver and Boyd Letters, Acc. 5000, Box 1, National Library of Scotland.

[55]The history of this case depends on which sources are taken seriously, for Galt and Horton had totally different versions. See Galt to Horton, Oct. 4, 1826, Colonial office (CO) 42/380, Public Record Office (PRO). Horton wrote Bathurst that the claimant's claims should be liquidated "although your Lordship will naturally be skeptical with respect to any proposition that may come from Mr. Galt," July 12, 1826, *Ibid.*

[56]Minutes of Court of Directors, Aug. 24, 1826, 1-17, CCP, PAO.

[57]Strachan to Galt, Sept. 25, 1826, enclosed with Strachan to Maitland Dec. 26, 1827,CO 42/383, PRO. Galt later admitted that "I was not aware of the virulence of party spirit in Canada. Never being a political man, the dissensions there did not attract my attention; I looked on them in some sort as borough squabbles, at most as a puddle in a storm." *Autobiography,* vol. I, 291.

[58]*Autobiography,* vol. I, 334.

[59]George S. Tiffany, Report of the Inspection of a block. . .Feb. 5, 1827, CCP Correspondence, PAO.

[60]Galt to Directors, Dec. 26, 1826, CCP Corres., PAO. *Letters from the Levant,* 291-292.

[61]Galt to Dunlop, Mar. 19, 1827, Galt Letters, PAO.

[62]William Dunlop to Thomas Ridout, April 10, 1827, Canada Company Papers, Crown Lands Department, Record Group 1, PAO. also, Charles Prior, "Report of the opera-

tion and the progress of Guelph," Oct. 1, 1827, CCC Corres., PAO. Prior's report is reprinted in Gilbert A. Stelter, "Charles Prior's report of the founding of Guelph," *Historic Guelph*, vol. 21 (July, 1982), 39-62.

[63]Galt to Directors, April 7, 1827, CCP Corres., PAO.

[64]*Autobiography*, vol. II, 53.

[65]Galt to Horton, Feb. 5, April 7, 1827, CO42/408, PRO.

[66]William Dickson to Col. W. Clause, Oct. 20, 1817, William Dickson Collection in possession of Mary Dickson Gindl, Blair, Ontario.

[67]This orientation was particularly apparent on the map which Galt was using early in 1827. "A map of the province of Upper Canada...compiled by James G. Chewett...and Thomas Ridout...Shewing the Districts Townships and Counties in which are situated the Lands purchased from the Crown by the Canada Company," Rare Map Collection, UGA.

[68]*Autobiography*, vol. II, 58-59.

[69]*Ibid.*, 54.

[70]For example, Galt to David Moir, April 30, 1827, Galt Papers, PAC.

[71]Galt to Directors, April 30, 1827, CCP Corres., PAO.

[72]*Autobiography*, vol. II, 54.

[73]*Pictures, historical and biographical, drawn from English, Scottish and Irish history* (London: Phillips, 1821), vol. II, 425. The title is somewhat misleading in that the work has more than 1000 pages of text.

[74]Minutes of the Court of Directors, July 6, 1827, CCP, PAO.

[75]Galt to Directors, July 12, 1827, CCP, Corres., PAO.

[76]Testimony published in *Court of Chancery of Upper Canada, 1853-4* (Toronto: Rowsell, 1854), vol. 4, 650.

[77]Galt to Directors, April 30, 1827, CCP, Corres., PAO.

[78]*Ibid.*, June 14, 1827.

[79]The earliest available drawn plan until recently was dated 1829, "Plan of Guelph," Baldwin Room, Metropolitan Toronto Public Library. But the 1829 portion was in fact an overlay of McDonald's 1828 plan, added after Galt's departure. This map was designated as an exhibit in the 1853 court case between the company and the town, and my sorting out of these maps depends in part on the evidence in this case.

[80]Published in Joseph Bouchette, *The British Dominions in North America* (London: Longman, 1831), vol. II, 60-61

[81]*Autobiography*, vol. II, 60-61.

[82]W.H. Playfair, *Report to the Right Honorable Lord Provost, Magistrates and Council of the City of Edinburgh...on a Plan for Laying out the New Town between Edinburgh and Leith* (Edinburgh: Smellie, 1819), 4.

[83]For detailed discussions of this phase of Edinburgh planning see Peter Reed, "Form and Context: a Study of Georgian Edinburgh," in Thomas A. Markus, ed., *Order in Space and Society: Architectural Form and its Context in the Scottish Enlightenment* (Edinburgh: Mainstream, 1982), 115-154, and A.J. Youngson, *The Making of Classical Edinburgh* (Edinburgh: University of Edinburgh Press, 1966).

[84]*Autobiography*, vol. II, 85.

[85]An excellent account of this tradition is in John Reps, *Town Planning in Frontier America* (Princeton: Princeton University Press, 1969), 295-99, 350-53.

[86]*Autobiography*, vol. II, 90.

[87]"Prior's Report," 47.

[88]Alexander Dunlop to his wife, June 15, 1827, published in A.E. Byerly, *The beginning of things in Wellington and Waterloo Counties with particular reference to Guelph, Galt and Kitchener* (Guelph: Guelph Publishing, 1935), 75.

[89]Galt to Jeannie Spirling, Nov. 28, 1827, Lizars Collection, UGA.
[90]Galt to Directors, May 31, 1827, CCP, Corres., PAO.
[91]"Prior's Report," 52.
[92]Galt to Jeannie Spirling, Nov. 28, 1827, Lizars Collection, UGA.
[93]Letter by Galt to anonymous friend, June 2, 1827, published in an article, "Guelph in Upper Canada," *Fraser's Magazine*, vol. 2 (November, 1830), 456.
[94]Directors to Galt, Sept. 24, 1827, CCP, Corres., PAO, and Galt to Directors, Jan. 5, 1828, *Ibid.*
[95]John Easthope to Galt, Nov. 6, 1828, *Ibid.*
[96]Changes on the 1828 map in the Baldwin Room, MTPL, are pencilled in. On later maps, in 1843 and 1847, the lines are drawn in. The company, however, lost the court case with the town over the ownership of the market ground.
[97]"Lands in Upper Canada to be disposed of by the Canada Company," February, 1833, Rare Map Collections, UGA. The subsequent history of Guelph is covered in C. Acton Burrows, *The annals of the town of Guelph, 1827-1877* (Guelph: Herald Stream Printing, 1877), and Leo A. Johnson, *History of Guelph 1827-1927* (Guelph: Guelph Historical Society, 1977). That of the Huron Tract is best related in Thelma Coleman and James Anderson, *The Canada Company* (Stratford: County of Perth and Cumming Publishers, 1978).
[98]Galt to Dalhousie, June 21, 22, 1828, John Galt Letters, Dalhousie Papers, Scottish Record Office.
[99]Galt to Dalhousie, Aug. 13, 1828, *Ibid.*
[100]Galt to Dalhousie, July 2, Aug. 23, 1833; Dalhousie to Galt, Aug. 13, 1833, *Ibid.* This story is told in detail in H.B. Timothy, *The Galts, a Canadian Odyssey* (Toronto: McClelland and Stewart, 1984), vol. II.
[101]*Autobiography,* vol. II, 63.
[102]*Lawrie Todd,* "Preface to the first edition."
[103]*Bogle Corbet,* vol. III, 30-31.
[104]Ironically, Ayn Rand's opening question in *Atlas Shrugged* (New York: Random House, 1957) — "Who is John Galt?" is answered by a description of a modern tycoon who believes in untrammelled self-interest.
[105]I have dealt with this early period in "The political economy of the city-building process: early Canadian urban development," in D. Fraser and A. Sutcliffe, eds., *The pursuit of urban history* (London: Arnold, 1983), reprinted in Gilbert A. Stelter and Alan F.J. Artibise, eds., *The Canadian city: essays in urban history,* 2nd. ed., (Ottawa: Carleton University Press, 1984), 4-30.
[106]See Gilbert Stelter, "Combining town and country planning in Upper Canada: William Gilkison and the Founding of Elora," in A.A. Brookes, ed., *The country town in rural Ontario's past* (Guelph: University of Guelph, Division of Continuing Education, 1981), 1-25.
[107]A point well made in Elizabeth Waterston's introduction to a reprinting of part of *Bogle Corbet* (Toronto: McClelland and Stewart, 1977), 1-7.

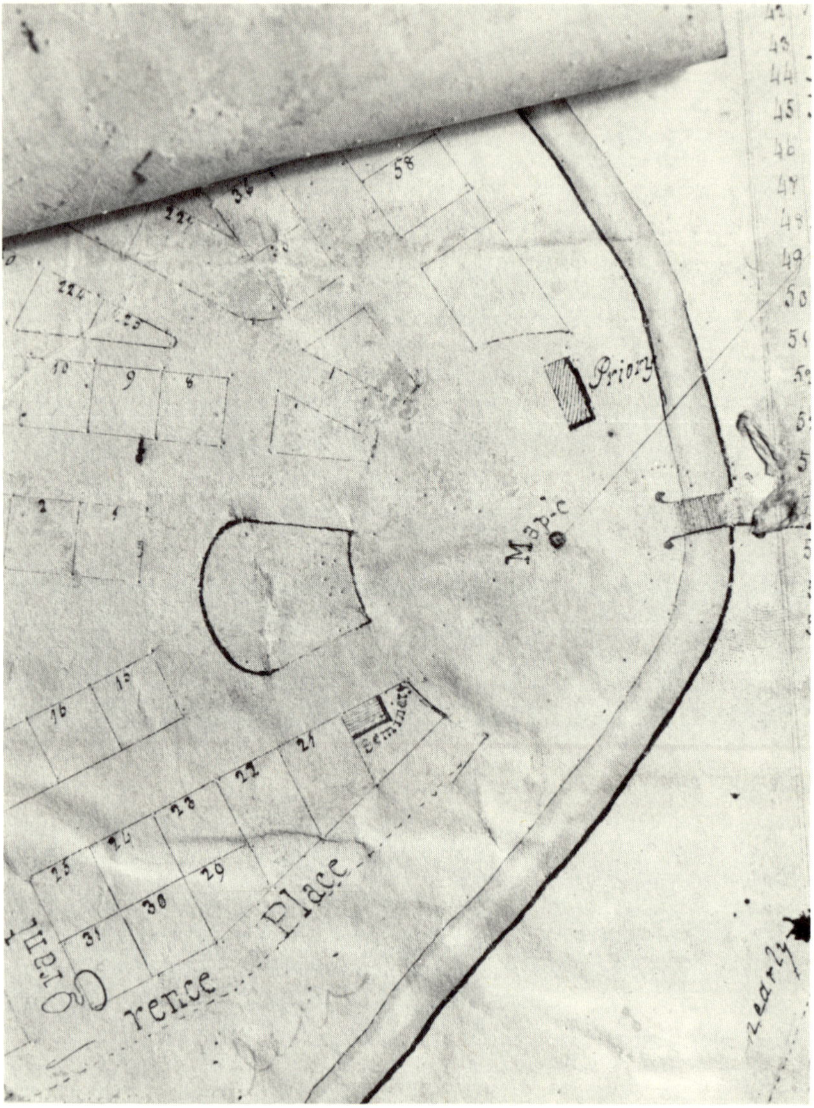

Plan No. 1: *Part of Guelph, 1828*

Shown is "Priory Place," the earliest focal point, at the bend of the Speed River. Note the Priory — the immigrant reception house — and the stump of the maple tree, from which all the streets radiate symmetrically. This plan was drawn by John McDonald in 1828 from George Tiffany's 1827 original. An 1829 overlay, which hid this plan from view for more than 150 years, can be seen at the top.

Source: Baldwin Room, Metropolitan Toronto Public Library.

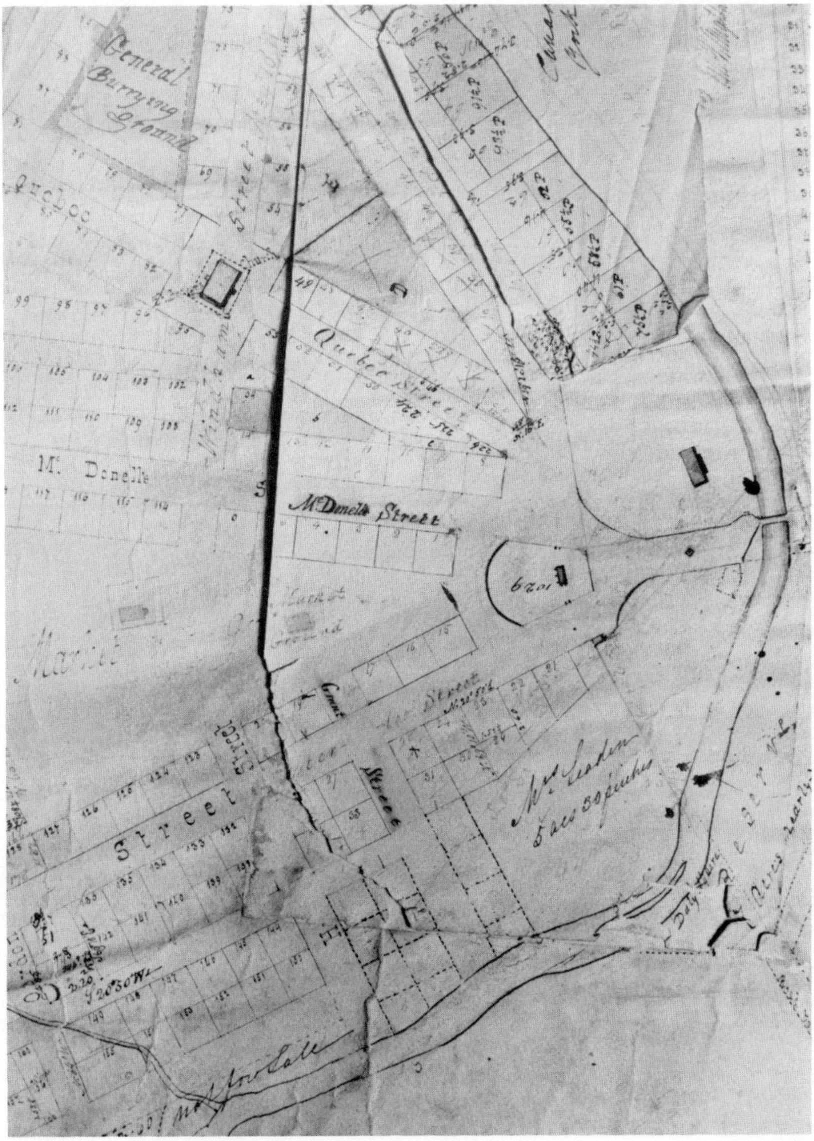

Plan No. 2: *Part of Guelph, 1829*

Clearly evident is the overlay which company officials placed on the plan in April, 1829. The symmetry of "Priory Place" was destroyed by the enclosure of public space. Streets now connect rather awkwardly with the focal point. The dotted lines of the attempted enclosure of the market ground are only faintly seen.

Source: Baldwin Room, Metropolitan Toronto Public Library.

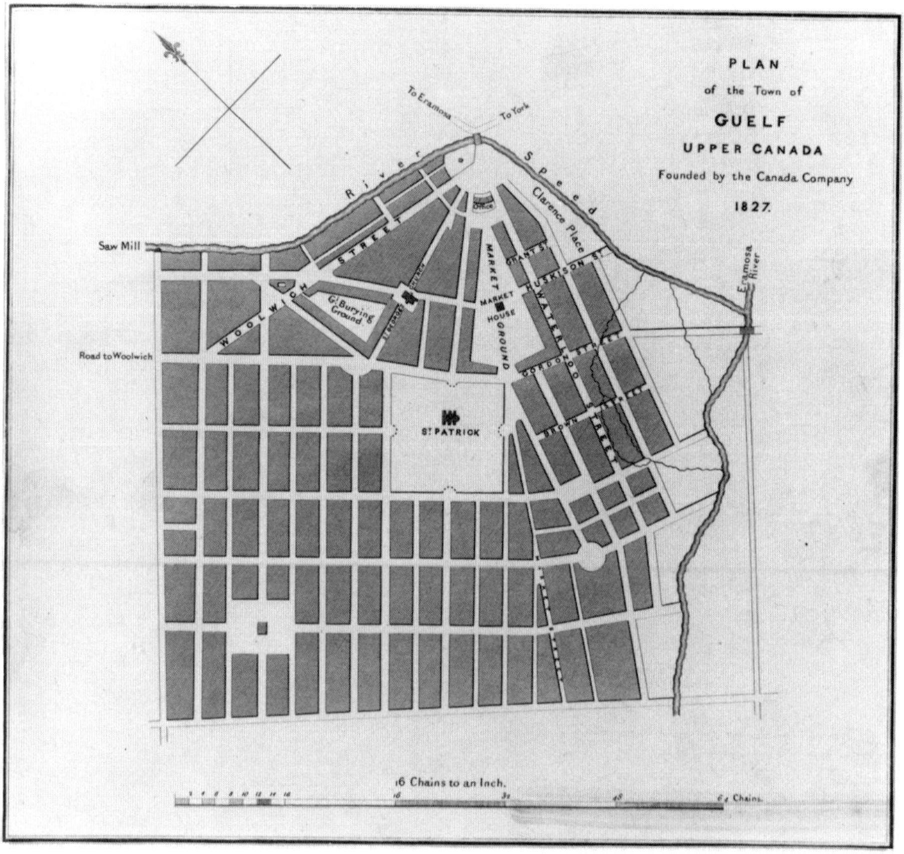

Plan No. 3: *Plan of Guelph, c.1828*

Shown is a conception of the total townsite, only part of which had been surveyed and cleared when this plan was drawn. Note the symmetrical character of "Priory Place" and the streets radiating from it; the generous size of the market ground; the enormous space granted to St. Patrick's Catholic Church; the square for St. George's Anglican Church; and the rather awkward connections between the radial and grid patterns. This engraving was based on a lithograph published by the Company for promotional purposes. In general terms it accurately portrayed the 1828 plan.

Source: Joseph Bouchette, *The British Dominions in North America* (London: 1831), Vol. I, p. 118.

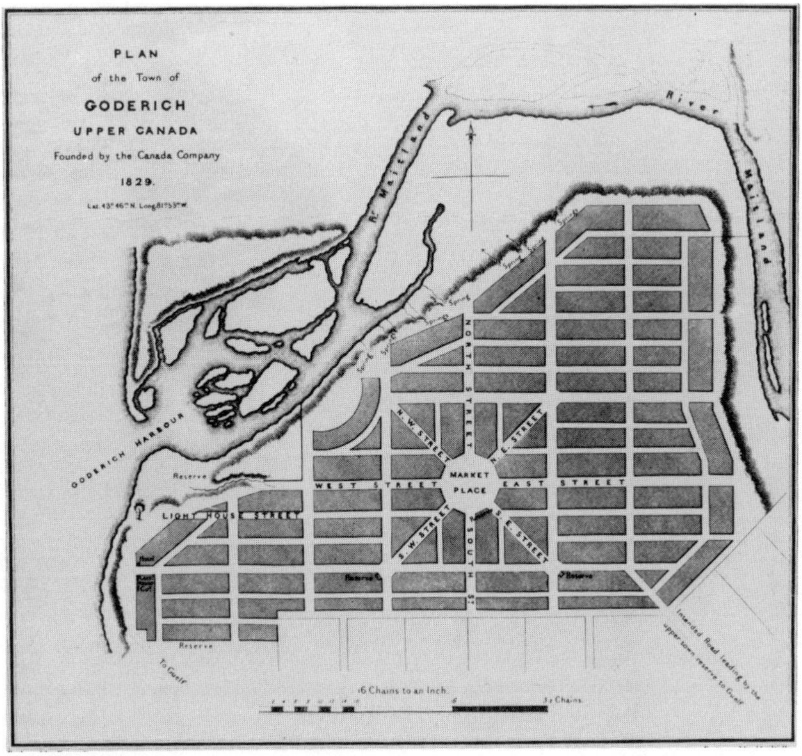

Plan No. 4: *Plan of Goderich, 1829*

Galt was also responsible for this plan, in which the interesting focal point, with its radial pattern, is effectively combined with the surrounding grid.

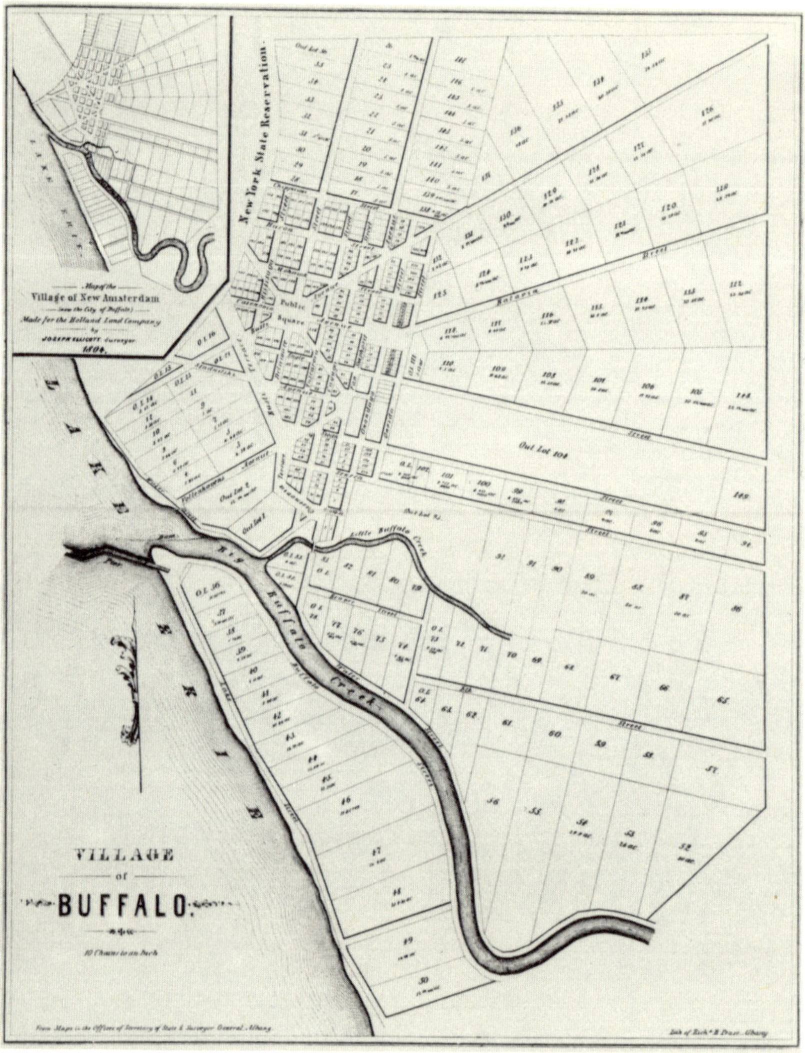

Plans Nos. 5 and 6: *Buffalo, 1804, and Indianapolis, 1821*

These are examples of Washington-inspired plans which may have influenced Galt's plans of Guelph and Goderich.

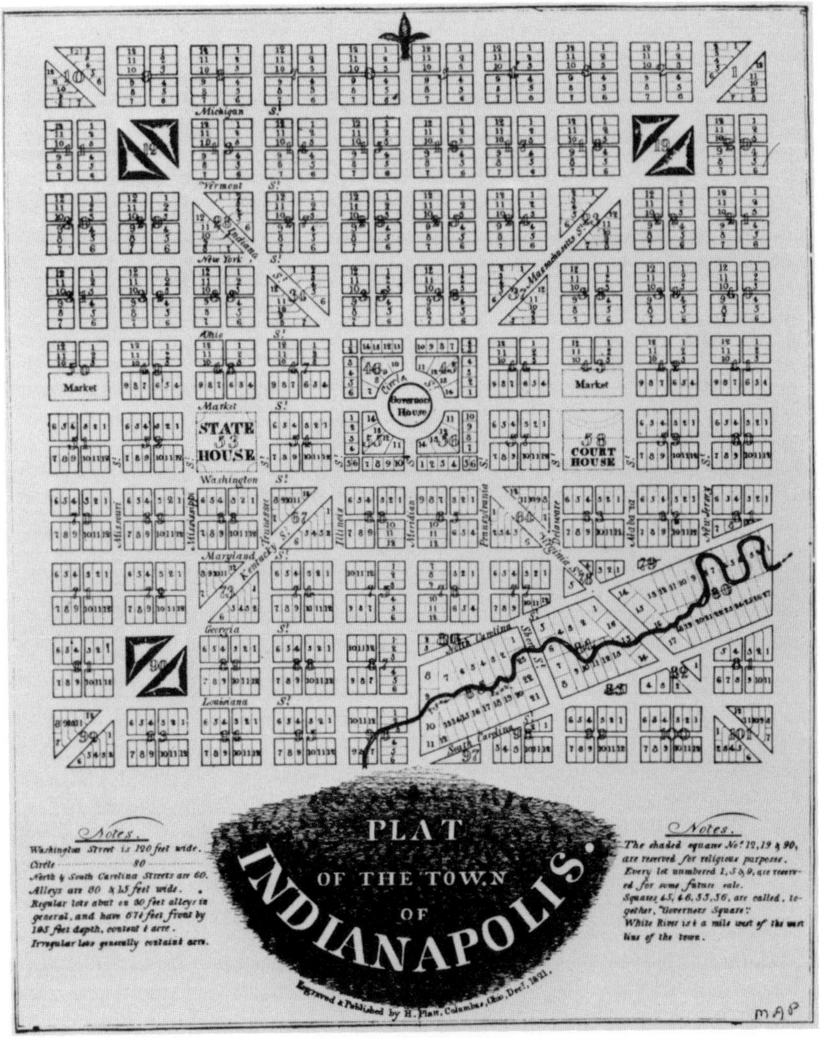

PLAT
OF THE TOW.N
OF
INDIANAPOLIS.
Notes.
Washington Street is 120 feet wide.
Circle 80
North & South Carolina Streets are 60.
Alleys are 30 & 15 feet wide.
Regular lots abut on 30 feet alleys in general, and have 67½ feet front by 195 feet depth, content ¼ acre.
Notes.
The shaded squares No.s 12, 19 & 90, are reserved for religious purposes.
Every lot numbered 1, 5 & 9, are reserved for some future sale.
Squares 45, 46, 55, 56, are called, together, "Governors Square".
White River is ¼ a mile west of the west line of the town.
Engraved & Published by H. Platt, Columbus, Ohio, Decr. 1821.
Market
STATE HOUSE
COURT HOUSE
Governors House

Galt's life and the *Autobiography*

Nick Whistler

Knowing the prosaic reasons why any man chose not just to live but also to write his life is a key to establishing the degree of surface or factual truth in an autobiography. Every autobiographer has a particular primary purpose when sitting down to write, a purpose which forms the basis of the process of selection.

Galt certainly had all the usual reasons and motives for writing an autobiography. The following passage from *The Omen* reveals that he had the necessary predeliction for the past:

> Some feel that their consciousness of life is in their recollections, others enjoy it in their anticipations. I am of those whose sense of being is derived from the past. Were the ever-forward-going mind a thing to be spoken of as having form and lineament, I should say, that the eyes of mine were in the back of the brain.[1]

He also owned to a poetic nature, and as Schiller said to Goethe:

> It is a need of poetic natures, if not of the human spirit altogether, to appropriate through their feelings as much world as is at all possible. (Letter to Goethe of September 7th, 1797)

Galt not only had the necessary desire to appropriate and possess life, he also suffered recurrent illnesses which made him highly aware of his own mortality. In 1833 the need to preserve something of himself — "to make a home for himself on paper"[2] impelled him to write an autobiography.

The commonest and ugliest reasons for writing one's life are egotism, a need for cash, and the lack of anything better to do. Galt faces such motives squarely. In his "Preface" he says that he writes because illness has resulted in "inability to employ himself in other pursuits than in those of literature." In that Galt gives the impression that the *Autobiography* is to be his last book, the phrase is an interesting echo of his comment on his first production: *The battle of Largs,* he says, was produced for "sheer want of something else to do."[3] He deflects the two other main criticisms of the autobiographer in the first sentence of his book, hoping to win the reader's sympathy by "candour":

> It is certainly not a very gentlemanly occupation to write one's own life; "my poverty not my will consents" to the egotistical undertaking.

Galt may have included such phrases, and the humiliating story of his time in debtors' prison, to distract readers from an investigation of his deeper financial motives.[4] In the last years of his life he had petitioned the government to pay him a commission for arranging the sale of Crown lands to the Canada Company, and perhaps he hoped that his picture of himself in the *Autobiography* as an ill-used, good-natured, and dying man would provoke a sympathetic response and increase the pressure on the government to grant his petition. If so, as happened all too often when he tried to influence politicians, his plan had the opposite effect, and his petition (*Autobiography* Vol. I, p. 296-308) was thrown out in 1834, shortly after the publication of his *Autobiography.*

Neither the obvious desire for royalties nor the hidden desire to influence politicians was his central purpose in writing the *Autobiography.* His main conscious aim was to fight back at the Canada Company, to prove to posterity that he should not have been "let go", and that he was a more creative, righteous, and honourable man than those who owned and controlled the company in 1833. The protagonist he created, the literary shape of the book, the principles of selection he employed and the energy with which he wrote all stem from outrage at his treatment by the Company. Galt was confident that his literary reputation was secure, but it was extremely important to his sense of self that his importance as a nation-builder should be acknowledged.[5] His comment that "when my numerous books are forgotten, I shall yet be remembered"[6] was made not because he thought that his books *would* be forgotten. Rather, it stemmed from his opinion mentioned twenty years earlier in the *Letters from the Levant* "that there is no permanent fame but that which is obtained by adding to the comforts of mankind" (p. 66). In the *Autobiography* Galt wished to prove that he had tried to add to mankind's physical as well as mental comforts. The reverses detailed in Galt's record of his career as a man of action were not all important to a man who wrote in his *Epistle to his sons on conduct*: "And yet not victory is the prize. . . for but the motive makes the hero great" (*Collected poems*, Vol. I ed. H.B. Timothy).

That Galt's main aim was to attack his enemies and to bolster his reputation is supported by the fact that he totally excludes his private life from the *Autobiography.* Reviewers at the time complained that "it is autobiography before the curtain,"[7] but I think that Galt remained before the curtain not because the stage was bare, but because he wished to focus attention on his business career. He gave a fuller account of his life as a writer in his second autobiography, the *Literary life,* but his decision to divide his account of himself into two parts continues to hamper a full evalutation of his motives and his eclectic but major contribution.

The hidden limits and direction of Galt's ambition are hinted at in *The Omen* when the author of that fictional autobiography says: "I felt, as it were, divine impulses, prompting me to holy enterprises — a light, a halo seemed to be shining around me" (p. 102). It seems odd to think of Galt's business career and the Canada Company as being — at least in the mind of its creator — a divinely predestined enterprise. We dismiss the idea because of the tendency to write off business as unromantic and unintellectual. Such an attitude ignores the fact that selfishness is one of the raw materials of human energy, and that much of humanity has long been engaged in business. The competitive desire for money and possessions — the profit motive — imparts an energy and creativity to business that is often underrated. The profit motive helped discover America, and put man on the moon and under the sea.

Yet trying to harness that motive for higher ends, as Galt at least partly did with the Canada Company, is rare. Such an effort is especially important in the Canadian context, for as Professor Symons observes of Canada, "there is no other country in the world, including the United States, where business has occupied a more central role in national development."[8] The period in which Galt was active in Upper Canada falls between the historically attractive and thus well-written-up events of the War of 1812 and the Rebellion of 1837, and Galt, well aware of the drawing power of "the bloody traditions of heroic lands" (Autobiography Vol. II, p. 103) would not have been surprised that his *Autobiography* has thus become one of the prime sourcebooks to a neglected but crucial period of Canadian history. He was well aware that "the general body of readers will regard his memoirs but as a common book, and never trouble themselves, in pursuit of pastime, to ascertain whether what they read consists of fact or fiction," (*Literary life*, Vol. I, p. 338). Because of the variety, quantity and reliability of untapped sources which cover the crucial part of Galt's *Autobiography* — his connection with the Canada Company — one is able to evaluate Galt's memory, methods and intentions to an unusual degree, from both the historical and literary perspectives. Because of his sense of the significance of his business career, Galt doubtless intended to tell the truth about his business life; but like most autobiographers, he tended to present the truth in its most winsome aspects. He improved on life — just as he asked the painter to lop ten years off his age when sitting for his portrait[9] — because his conscience allowed him to manipulate appearances if the end result was creative. For Galt, truth was at the service of

> every thing tending to preserve, heighten, and perpetuate, those public affections, which, although it has become fashionable to decry them as prejudices, are still the sources that contribute to, elevate, and sustain the dignity of nations. (*Letters from the Levant,* p. 349)

Galt was unusually aware that his prejudices and subconscious wishes sometimes clouded his judgement and interfered with his ability to tell the truth, as this passage from the *Literary life* demonstrates:

> I only propose to myself to give a fair description of facts as they happened, without intentionally biassing their impressions on the reader. The leaning of all men in their own favour is, I hope, not with me greater than with my neighbours, though it may probably be obviously enough strong to incline me in doubtful matters to think myself in the right. (*Literary life,* Vol. I, p. 34)

Galt knew that whether a lie is to the self or the world, whether it is told in public or in the family circle or in a book, whether it is a lie of exaggeration, a barefaced lie or — hardest to detect — a lie of omission, untruth has a power or virulence that varies in degree according to the situation in space and in time, and to the cultural and religious assumptions of the day. The belief that truth needed to be fought for (and that the reward might be in heaven) was unusually strong in Galt's own Presbyterian and Scottish background, and in the public life and scientific research of his day.[10]

The doctrine of predestination — the idea that one's place in life and the after-life is decided by God before birth — is perhaps the most distinctive concept of the Presbyterian faith in which Galt was brought up. Galt says that he included his play *The star of destiny in the Autobiography* simply because his life story had run a bit shorter than expected, and he wished "to give the reader his full pennyworth." (*Autobiography,* Vol. II, p. 373) Maybe, maybe...

Besides making adjustments to the truth because of his focus on his business career, and because of his concern with encouraging "public affections", Galt wrote because he was accustomed to writing. But his professional competence produced problems for him as an autobiographer, as the ability to exaggerate, fictionize, and to manipulate the reader is highly developed in professional writers, and their autobiographies are thus especially suspect. As the product of one of the most prolific and inventive manipulators of the autobiographic genre, Galt's autobiography must be even more carefully evaluated than the life stories of most authors. Galt not only wrote dozens of fictional autobiographies and his own autobiography twice, but included the real autobiography of another man in one of his fictional autobiographies, and, in "translating" Alfieri's autobiography he rewrote it, including his own experiences and imposing his own values on the book.[11]

One of the most glaring reasons for suspecting the version of the self presented in any self-portrait is the obvious distortion that comes about when anyone tries to reduce a whole waking and dreaming life into something that takes but a few hours to read. A professional "autobiography" writer such as Galt had had much more practice than most autobiographers at conjuring up memory, and at the process of selection and reduction, and thus has a much greater control over the self-image he presents to his reader. Galt was also well aware of the effects of time on memory, as the following passage from his book *The Omen* indicates.

> Sometimes, on the revisitations of the past, strange and obscure apparitional resemblances leave me in doubt whether they are indeed the memory of things which have been, or but of the stuff that dreams are made of. (p.1)

The autobiographer has none of the usual devices of fiction for gripping the reader. There is always one main character in an autobiography, and to be read

— to sell — that character *must* be compelling. To sell a lot of copies over time, the protagonist has to conform to mass appeal archetypes or stereotypes, and thus the author is usually forced to exaggerate, to paint himself as super-rich or super-adventurous. But Galt's forte in fiction had been the creation of atypical protagonists. He also felt that his life could provide material for that rare text, a successful autobiography; when discussing his *Autobiography* in the *Literary life,* he mentions that his "own adventures were as singular as those of the heroes of many novels. . ." Galt's experiences had also made him aware that in autobiography understatement appears to denote modesty; so in his own autobiography he chose a plain clear style and adopted an anti-heroic stance to give the impression that his protagonist was a modest but true hero. Galt also establishes in the "Preface" that his career is over. He exploits the reader's tendency to believe that one who has retired from the competition of life, where a competent and confident facade must be presented to the world, no longer needs to maintain that facade and is thus, in retirement, freer to speak truth.

Finally, professional writer's vanity makes Galt particularly suspect when he portrays himself as a "brilliant" writer — one who requires only a single draft to provide good copy — rather than as a "craftsman" whose genius lies in revision and editing. Galt tells us that he is dictating from his sickbed, sending each sheet to be set in print as it is finished. If we believe him, we must be amazed at his facility and power of composition. If we do not take his word for it, and find that he wrote, rewrote, edited and corrected his life as some clues suggest,[12] our sense of the general tenor of the man's mind, and of his true self, would be significantly changed.

The deathbed scene is the time when the veil is often drawn back, and a person's inner character and beliefs are revealed. Galt placed an account of his own deathbed scene in the *Autobiography,* and wrote of himself in the "Preface" in the third person and past tense, concluding "The memoir terminates with his last imminent illness." The conclusion to the whole autobiography is a protracted deathbed scene, with recoveries and relapses, ending with a image of his own end as:

> something like a cat that I was at the drowning of in my boyish years: — a country carter, who looked over my shoulder at the sight, on seeing the poor animal, remarked on the catastrophe, that it would "take pains to kill her."

Galt's portrait of himself on his deathbed in the *Autobiography* is endearing — one senses courage and humour in the "levity" of his tone — but it is extremely manipulative of the reader's sympathy. Galt himself hints that his light tone is but one side of the coin: "I seemingly speak of the event [his death] with levity, but really do not pretend to look on the King of Terrors with less awe than my neighbours." (*Autobiography,* Vol. II, p. 286)

Luckily there is another, that is to say a non-Galtian account of Galt's actual death, by a Reverend Mr. Gilmour. Professor Ian Gordon modestly mentions his discovery of Gilmour's account in a footnote and also notes that Moir, Galt's friend, doctor and biographer, had the account but did not use it! Clearly Moir felt that Galt's version in his own *Autobiography* was for some reason preferable.

Professor Gordon reports:

Mr. Gilmour firmly wrote in his narrative that Galt. . . confessed himself a lost and hopeless sinner in the sight of God, professed his faith in Christ as the only, the appointed, the All-sufficient Saviour: declared his belief in the written word of God as at once the warrant and the rule of his faith; and expressed his entire dependance on the Holy Spirit to regenerate, to sanctify, and to save. (*Life of a writer,* p. 154-5)

Gordon, suggesting that the account is unreliable, adds as a postscript "It reads like one of the horror scenes from *The Entail.*" Yet Harriet Pigott's eyewitness account in the Pigott manuscripts at the Bodleian library makes clear that Gilmour was not alone. In her manuscript biography — compiled with Galt's help — she notes "To pervert and misrepresent his principles on the essential point of religion raucous attempts have been made and by his own countrymen." (p. 158)

Carlyle asserts in *On heroes* that "a man's religion is the chief fact with regard to him." He goes on to say that by religion "I do not mean here the church creed which he professes. But the thing a man does practically believe. . . concerning his vital relations to this mysterious universe. . . is in all cases the primary thing for him, and creatively determines all the rest." ("The hero as divinity") The sense of a particular man's "religion" is very hard to develop, but such a sense is the best guide through the maze of the suspect self presented in the *Autobiography.*

Galt's true belief about his "vital relations to this mysterious universe" is very important because of its bearing on the sort of power he wished to have in the real world of business and colonization, and on the power he wished to wield with his pen — the morals he wished to inculcate with his fables. But establishing what Galt's "religion" actually was is especially difficult, as he tended to speak freely only in his anonymous fiction (and perhaps, as Dr. Timothy has suggested, in his poetry). The impression given at the surface level in the *Autobiography* is that of a sophisticated anti-sectarian agnostic of a scientific cast of mind, who refers to the Christian God as if deferring to the custom of the day. He never mentions attending church, though none of his critics seem to have commented on that fact.

Galt's interest in explaining coincidences also leads one to a fuller sense of his religion. He reveals one of his main reasons for writing the *Autobiography* early in the first volume:

This incident (regarding Upper Canada) is, in itself, not deserving of notice, but as a link in an important chain it merits serious attention; few biographical sketches with which I am acquainted, present, indeed, such a series of transactions, that so well deserve the epithet of fatal, in the philosophical sense of the term. (*Autobiography,* Vol. I, p. 98)

This passage is intriguing: I had often noticed that whenever Galt uses jerky syntax and many commas as in the above passage, such stylistic mannerisms are indicators of strong feeling.

Having decided that the sceptical scientific tone of the protagonist in the *Autobiography* was on some level false, I dug deeper, still seeking "the thing a man does practically believe. . .(which) determines all the rest." I had noticed Galt's recurrent use of the word "bodements," which appeared in the context of similar stylistic mannerisms to those noted in the above passage on coincidence. When Galt used this word in the Canadian passages it appeared side by side with such comments as: "the founding of a town was certainly one of [those occasions]. . .of which a horoscope might be cast" (*Autobiography* Vol. II p. 54). I was led by this reference to horoscopes to glance at his book *The Omen* (of which he revealed his authorship in the *Autobiography,* smugly noting that many had ascribed the novella to Walter Scott). At the beginning of Epoch I, Chapter VI, he asks a general question about "bodements".

Why are we so averse to confess to one another, how much we in secret acknowledge to ourselves, that we believe the mind to be endowed with other faculties of perception than those of the corporeal senses? We deride with worldly laughter the fine enthusiasm of the conscious spirit that gives heed and credence to the metaphorical intimations of prophetic reverie, and we condemn as superstition, the faith which consults the omens and oracles of dreams.

One cannot say unequivocally that this belief in omens represents Galt's point of view, since the passage is included in a fictional autobiography. However the remarks are followed by a passage of extraordinary insight, and one again senses the real Galt revealing his essential beliefs:

It may be that the soul never sleeps, and what we call dreams, are but the endeavours which it makes, during the trance of the senses, to reason by the ideas of things associated with the forms and qualities of those whereof it then thinks. Are not indeed the visions of our impressive dreams often but the metaphors with which the eloquence of the poet would invest the cares and anxieties of our waking circumstances and rational fears?

Galt's speculations about the sources of "bodements" and the purpose of dreams pre-date Freud's insights by almost a century. Given that Freud had trouble gaining respect for his ideas then, it is not surprising that Galt ends the passage with a disclaimer:

These reflections, into which I am perhaps too prone to fall, partake somewhat of distemperature and disease. . .

I said "ends the passage", but the sentence is one of Galt's many false endings. Having disarmed his reader by acknowledging that such ideas are but "lunacies of the imagination" he continues:

> But they are not therefore the less deserving of solemn consideration... Nor is it wise in considering the state and frame of man to overlook how much the universal element of disease affects the evolutions of fortune. Madness often babbles truths which make wisdom wonder.

This idea that the mad are often wise recurs again and again in Galt's work.

Finally hoping to see if Galt made any comments on his unorthodox occult beliefs under his own name, I glanced through the carefully provided chapter headings in the *Literary life.* A whole chapter on witchcraft! and Galt in his own voice saying:

> I may as well state my peculiar notions on witchcraft, not that I can expect many to agree with me... I have, however, to confess, admitting the qualification to be afterwards mentioned, that I have, down to the period of this present writing, been always a believer in the art...[13]

and:

> Of the existence of a class of criminals, conscious of possessing an ascendency over the timid and credulous I have no doubt; and it is necessary to deter them from practicing their sleights, that I conceive the laws against witchcraft should not have been repealed. I know a gentleman intimately of no ordinary accomplishment, who regarded another as the demon of his fate, and never met him without viewing, as he thought, some secret admonition of misfortune that would ensue. Had he... known... (and had he used his knowledge) he would have been what the law considered a wizard. (*Literary life* p. 69-70)

Galt also refers to demons of fate — bad luck visitors — in *The Omen* (p. 22) and in *Letters from the Levant*[14] and he concludes the chapter on witchcraft as follows:

> I am... persuaded that there is more in the gossipry about the influence of the evil eye, and the good and bad luck of certain visitors, than is dreamt of in philosophy. (*Literary life* p. 70)

I think that Galt gave but the surface impression of himself and his religion and motivations in the *Autobiography* because he wished to reach as wide an audience as possible, one that generally saw reason and religion (let alone business) as oil and water, immiscible. Thus in reading and evaluating the *Autobiography* one must pay extremely close attention if one is to correctly evaluate the literary self-myth of one of the greatest of first person myth makers. If "autobiography is [to be used as] a valuable corrective to historiography,"[15] and if "the historian can only reconstruct the past by borrowing from and applying his own experience of life"[16] then "only those who have had the experience of examining and feeling their own dreams and have learned what exists in their emotional inwardness within their personal abysses, can objectively attempt to look at what issues from the inwardness of others."[17]

In examining Galt's "issue" one must therefore not only check the truth of matters of fact, but also note repetitions — such as "bodements" — rhythms, punctuation, and the sort of errors to which Freud assigned the name parapraxes.

Galt himself gives one an excellent example of how a one-letter misprint to some degree changed his direction in life:

About this time I had several works in hand, and was over head and ears in the depths of Gothic antiquities, some how prompted by Pinkerton's Dissertation and Mallet's Researches. However, I was providentially rescued by an error of the press, when I transmitted a lucubration to the Edinburgh Magazine, to which Park and I became stealthy contributors. It was a most recondite essay on Polytheism, in which an essential name was wrong spelt; the mistake, *though but in one letter,* was so absurd, that it brought on such a fit of laughing, by which all my antiquarian vapours were dispersed, and I never could abide to think of the subject with gravity enough to resume it afterwards. The essay, with all its imperfections on its head, is the October number of the year 1802. (*Autobiography,* Vol. 1, p. 56)

The possible importance of such "errors" to an understanding of the man is demonstrated by the fact that a minute check of the essay in question ("Of the Origin of Polytheism" *Scots Magazine,* November *not* October, 1802) reveals no such misprint.

I will conclude this essay by presenting my annotations to a brief section of the *Autobiography* in the hope that they will aid further speculation about the way Galt transmitted life into the strange brew of art and history which constitutes autobiography. The passage forms the last sentence of the climactic chapter of the *Autobiography,* which describes the founding of Guelph.

But Guelph, to resume a little more freedom,[a] was, like all cities fated[b] with a high destiny, the cause of quarrels; Romulus slew his brother for hopping over the walls of Rome,[c] and although the history of my city is not likely to be honoured[d] by warlike events, it yet gave rise to a controversy as worthy[e] of commemoration, for from the day that I announced the birth[f] of this metropolis to the directors of the Canada Company, my troubles and vexations began, and were accumulated on my unsheltered head till they could be no longer endured.[g]

a. Galt uses the phrase "resume a little more freedom" as a linking device at the moment he wishes to turn from specifics to generalities, and perhaps because he is subconsciously aware that he is making free with the classical myth. The word is also a sign that he is about to end the chapter with one of his habitual long accelerating and progressively strident sentences of complaint.

b. A close reading of Galt's seven versions of the founding of Guelph reveal that Galt made every attempt to ensure that his city was "fated." He admits that "it was consistent with |his| plan to invest our ceremony with a little mystery, the better to make it remembered." He talks of the founding of a town as a moment at "which a horoscope might be cast," and he chose to found the town on St. George's Day "which secretly I was determined should be so celebrated as to be held in remembrance, and yet so conducted as to be only apparently accidentally impressive." Not wishing to reveal these plans to the business interests back home he lies to them, and in his report states that "By an agreeable and unforseen circumstances the first tree was felled on St. George's Day."

c. Galt's introduction of this Roman myth is interesting in light of several points: his reference earlier in the chapter to himself and his companion Dr. Dunlop as the "Babes in the Woods," and to his "excessive anger" with Dunlop; the likening of his alter ego Lawrie Todd to one of the Babes; the allusion to the desire of one of the party in the town founding expedition in *Laurie Todd* to murder the other Babe in that account, Bailie Waft, who has much in common with Dunlop; and the comment by Bruno Bettelheim that fairy tales (and, it has been suggested, myths such as Romulus and Remus) mirror the child's desire to split the self into two, to distance the self from the part that has misbehaved. I found a strongly anti-Roman article which I believe to be by Galt in *Fraser's Magazine* (October, 1837) which begins with a quotation from *Coriolanus:* "I would not be a Roman, of all nations; I had as lieve be a condemned man."

d. The tone of the word "honoured" is important; much of Galt's life and work was aimed at proving that the hierarchy of male heroism needed to be reversed, that the trader and town founder was more worthy of honour and hero-worship, and of the rank of *gentle*man, than the soldier. That Galt consciously aimed to create new myths and role models and yet was fully aware of the attraction of the warrior hero shows in his use of the word "legends" in the following passage:

> The transactions |at Guelph| will be, however, memorable in the history of what must be a great country, and neither open enmity, nor the covert machinations of personal malice, nor the ingenuity of sordid self-interest, can hereafter prevent my humble name from being associated with the legends of undertakings at least as worthy of commemoration as the bloody traditions of heroic lands. (*Autobiography* Vol. II, p. 103-104).

Galt's rejection of the general notion of what makes an "honourable" man was in many ways similar to Wordsworth's, and though Galt had initially been in favour of liberalisation, the events in France proved to him that his early liberalism and "military ardour" was misplaced. He came to recognise that

we are in society, held together by ties more slender than we are willing to believe. The dissolution of the social order by the French revolution has given a lesson that has not sufficiently been studied. (*Autobiography* Vol. I, p. 92)

Perhaps this comment inspired Carlyle (who wrote his own autobiography at the same time) to action. Galt's re-ordering of the male hierarchy of heroism — placing philanthropists highest, poets and mythmakers second, and soldiers last — did not happen so as to justify his anti-heroic stance in the *Autobiography*. (e.g. *Autobiography* Vol. I, p. 186). The first of the following two passages illustrates that his reordering of the three types of heroes happened early, and taken with the second excerpt proves that the Canada Company grew out of Galt's fame-oriented value system, that it was not a "mere land jobbing concern."

What a strange thing is glory! Little more than three hundred years ago all Christendom rang with the battle of Lepanto; and yet there seems to be a probability that it will be interesting to posterity only as forming an occurrence in the life of one of the privates engaged in it. This is certainly no very melancholy reflection; to me, indeed, it is an agreeable one; for I have begun to be of opinion, that there is no permanent fame but that which is obtained by adding to the comforts of mankind; and military transactions do not otherwise produce any thing in this way, but as furnishing topics which authors may manage in such a manner as to afford, in the perusal, the most interesting of all pastimes. Not that I think less of military virtues; on the contrary, I am the more convinced of their value and essentiality to the dignity of the human character. (*Letters from the Levant,* p. 66-67)

I. . .believe that there is truth in the old adage, which says, "the man who makes a blade of corn grow where it never did before, does more good to the world than did Julius Caesar." With this aim I have long been animated. (*Literary life,* Vol. I, p. 30)

e. The word "worthy" gives one an idea of Galt's estimate of his own achievements. Note that at the end of his life Galt says that "the object [of his life] has been in some degree attained" (*Literary life,* p. 55). His summation of his achievements in Canada in the *Autobiography* is also revealing:

My employment, as superintendent of the Canada Company, though not unmixed with the usual alloy which attends and troubles all human affairs, was congenial to my humour. I could desire none better, and though I may not be credited, had no wish for a lot of greater splendour. For my tasks were so evidently calculated to lessen the mass of afflictions, that, however teasing in the performance, they could not be contemplated without vivid delight. The emoluments were no doubt respectable, but I have ever regarded pecuniary matters as subordinate, and at that crisis, [his recall] if a thought gravitated down towards them, it was but for a moment, when I remembered my children. (*Autobiography* Vol. II, 153)

f. With the word "birth" the image of himself as father of Guelph is completed, with the Directors taking the place of his own disapproving parents. Something of Lear's feelings about his ungrateful progeny hangs about Galt's father image — he announces the birth of his city as the death of his own hopes.

g. Galt implies that he left the Company because *he* could not "endure" it. It is certainly true that he was recalled to London, but, according to Professor Roger Hall's 1973 University of Cambridge dissertation on the Canada Company, and to the Letterbooks in the Archives of Ontario, Galt does not seem to have been officially fired. His adversary Lieutenant-Governor Maitland was recalled for his injudicious conduct in the Forsyth case (O.D. Skelton, *Life of A.T. Galt,* p. 26) which must have given Galt a certain amount of cold comfort. I imagine, however that the address from his Guelph constituents "could not fail to have been exceeding gratifying to him," (Moir) and must have been one of the most treasured items in his possession. Though he mentions the incident in the *Autobiography* he did not include it as it would have clashed with the modest anti-heroic stance so necessary to obtaining the sympathy of his reader. The address runs as follows:

Sir, — We, the undersigned inhabitants of the town and township of Guelph, learning that are about to leave us, beg to express our sincere regret that we should be deprived of your presence, and the satisfaction and pleasure it has ever afforded us. We trust and hope that your absence from amongst us will not be of long duration, and that you will accomplish the objects of your journey, whatever these may be. We would wish to express to you the obligations which you have conferred upon us, in the prosperity which has flowed upon us ever since we became united with you and the Canada Company — many of us having come here in dependent circumstances, who are now in fair way to become independent, and all having improved their condition under your fostering care. By the measures you have adopted, our lands in many instances have, in the space of eighteen months, doubled or tripled their values; and we do not look on our obligations as the less, that the Canada Company has shared in the advantage. You have set an example to the province in the formation of proper roads and bridges, and showed by what means the progress of the settlement of the colony can be accelerated an hundredfold by your measures, which have created this town and township. Finally, we beg you to accept of our best wishes for your happiness and prosperity, wherever you may be; and we request you to thank the Canada Company for all the benefits they have conferred on us, and the greatest of these we consider their having sent you amongst us.

Signed by 144 heads of families. (Moir, *Biographical Memoir John Galt,* p. Lxxiii)

NOTES

[1]*The Omen.* Edinburgh: Blackwood, and London: T. Cadell, 1825, p. 16.

[2]Alfred Kazin, "The self as history" in *Telling lives* ed. Marc Pachter, Philadelphia: University of Pennsylvania, 1979.

[3]*The Autobiography of John Galt.* London: Cochrane and M'Crone, 1833, Vol. I, p. 73. The autobiography was edited and reprinted in *Greenbank's Periodical Library* published in Philadelphia in 1833.

[4]One of the reasons Galt fell into bad odour with the Canada Company Directors was because he tried to buy land from the Company, which, as he was an employee, went against company regulations. Galt's will does not exist, so the extent and origins of his land holdings in Canada (mentioned in the *Autobiography*) have been hard to verify. However Gloria Troyer of the University of Guelph Library drew my attention to a location ticket in the Samuel Street Papers, (the Goodwin Haines collection, Archival Collections, University of Guelph Library) which records that Galt was granted 1000 acres in Innisfil Township, and 200 acres in Tay Township by Thomas Ridout on the fifth of January, 1828.

[5]In his "American Traditions" article (*Fraser's Magazine,* October, 1830), Galt clearly admits that he aims to help found a new and authentically American literature. According to R.K. Gordon's research notes in the University of Calgary Archives Galt donated twelve volumes of his confidential American papers to the Greenock Library which if still in existence should throw more light on his understanding of the continent.

[6]*The literary life and miscellanies of John Galt* in three volumes. Edinburgh: Blackwood, 1834, Vol. I, p. 358.

[7]Mrs. Johnstone in the October 1833 issue of *Tait's Edinburgh Magazine,* quoted in Ian A. Gordon, *John Galt. The life of a writer* Toronto: University of Toronto Press, 1972, p. 116.

[8]Quoted by Roger D. Hall in "A Canadian context for business studies," *Canadian Issues* (Vol. 2, no. I) p. 53.

[9]Jennie W. Aberdein. *John Galt* Oxford University Press, 1936, p. 192.

[10]The popularity of Walter Scott's fables demonstrate the need for relief from this strict approach. Galt, always out of step, seems to be at his most fanciful when announcing his "scientific" achievements: "at last I hit upon what seemed as important a discovery as steam..." *Autobiography,* Vol. II, p. 150-151.

[11]This information is contained in a note on the inside front cover of Galt's unpublished translation of Alfieri's life, now in the John Galt papers in the Archives of Ontario.

[12]In my 1984 Guelph M.A. thesis "John Galt's *Autobiography:* Fact, Fiction and Truth," I include an appendix containing six other versions by Galt of the story of the founding of Guelph.

[13]*Literary life,* p. 68. N.B. Freud's assertion "Words and magic were in the beginning one and the same thing." (*A general introduction to psychoanalysis,* New York: Liverwright, 1935)

[14]He also comments that whereas Scots have second sight and Albanians second hearing, the English are "not free from a strange smell." (p. 179)

[15]Roy Pascal *Design and truth in autobiography,* Cambridge: Harvard University Press, 1960, p. 179-180.

[16]Marc Bloch quoted in C.V. Wedgewood *Truth and opinion,* London: Collins, 1960, p. 20.

[17]Leon Edel in *Telling lives,* p. 43.

Bogle Corbet and the annals of new world parishes.

Elizabeth Waterston

John Galt's novels anatomize the social community, and analyze the real urban pressures of his time. *Annals of the Parish* traces the metamorphosis of a loose rural community into a complex coherent town. *The Ayrshire Legatees* ironically follows a family from Scottish country life to London and back again. *The Provost* dissects the city as a political organism. *Sir Andrew Wylie* uses London as setting. The central character in The *Last of the Lairds* shuts down his rural heritage and moves to Edinburgh. As a book which is climaxed by the founding of a town, *Bogle Corbet* deserves attention because of its place in this sequence.

Bogle Corbet is also important because its fictional account of town-building can be matched against documentary records of the founding of Guelph, and against Galt's other account of his plans, actions, and achievements, presented in *The Autobiography*. There is stuff here for an interesting study in the processes of the creative imagination, a comparison between documented reports of circumstances, persons and events, and the transmuted forms of these, in fictional setting, characters, and plot.

A third claim to our attention is that in this novel John Galt found a form and a tone which not only caught his own experiences in small-town life in Canada, but which also remained appropriate for subsequent Canadian treatments of the same theme. Many later Canadian writers, from Stephen Leacock and L.M. Montgomery to Alice Munro and Margaret Laurence, would voice their own "annals of the parish" in a form similar to Galt's. Views of Canadian town life very similar to Galt's would re-surface in many later Canadian writers' work.

Galt worked as a pseudo-statistician, recording the minutiae of silting social and business and economic and theological changes in a complex human community — a town. Perhaps his focus on town annals was in part a reaction against the powerful romantic mystique of nature. When Scott or Wordsworth, Blake or Coleridge responded to the mystery, dignity and magical power of landscape, John Galt turned to the pleasures and humours of town life. Just glance at some contrasts between his life and Wordsworth's, for instance, for an illumination of the antithesis. Wordsworth was born in 1770, Galt in 1779. In *The Prelude,* Wordsworth records his boyhood experiences in nature; Galt in *The Autobiography* traces his business apprenticeship. As a young man the poet fled to the Lake country; Galt moved to Greenock,Paisley, Glasgow. At twenty-eight, Wordsworth wrote the personal, deeply meditative "Tintern Abbey: on revisiting the Banks of the Wye"; Galt at twenty-nine wrote *A statistical account of Upper Canada* — a cool, business-like report on a country he had not yet visited. At twenty-nine the poet settled in Grasmere; Galt at that same age moved to London. The great "Intimations Ode" crystallizes the Romantic religion of nature; Galt's novels form a realistic compendium on town life.

If this bias against solitude and nature stems in part from resistance to the literary fashion for solitary walks, cloud-like wandering, or rhapsodies on lochs, glens, and cataracts, it derives in part also from a deep-seated personal malaise in the presence of elemental forces. Galt's *Autobiography* begins with the memory of a picture of Niagara Falls. "My juvenile imagination was awfully excited," he says.[1] *Bogle Corbet* would work slowly up to a visit to the actual Falls: the famous mock-heroic passage describing Urseline Corbet's reaction reveals Galt's long-lasting inability to respond directly to that "awful" sight.[2] *The Autobiography* continues, "Till finally removed to Irvine, I have no particular recollection, except of a storm at sea, of which a description is given in the Provost" (I,9). That terrifying storm would recur, in *The Last of the Lairds* and *The Entail*. In *The Provost*, on a windy Yule, helpless boats are battered by "contrary winds"; mother and bairns pace the shores where fires burn; bodies are cast up by the waves.[3] In *The Entail*, young Walkinshaw on shore witnesses the shipwreck of his uncle. This ship is destroyed "as if made of glass"; fragments of the foam are covered with blood.[4] On shore, the storm has "the roar and rage of Niagara" (E, 319). *The Last of the Lairds*, climactically, shows the consuming destruction of the storm augmented by fire at sea; a madwoman cabins her babies in the fiery ship, while terrified survivors in the lifeboats chop off the hands of those in the water who clutch at the gunwales.[5] These cataclysmic scenes are increasingly peripheral to the main action of Galt's Scottish novels; understandably he pushes the terrifying elemental scenes to the margin of his reader's attention, while focusing on tamer, safer,domestic and social realities.

Passage to America would of course do nothing to allay Galt's obsessive fear of disaster on water. In *Lawrie Todd*, a storm stirs "the river black and sepulchral" into "ravenous whirlpools", and the waves carry a drunken woman in a scow to destruction.[6] *Bogle Corbet* returns to storm at sea. Near Anticosti, an island fraught with legends of cannibalism, Bogle and his group watch helplessly while their companion ship is driven ashore and wrecked.

Galt's terror in the face of nature, then, augments his desire to make a strong case for town life in the new world. The desire to chop down trees, dam up the river, and above all to bind human lives together like a "bundle of sticks" illustrates a set of attitudes which would become very common in Canada — attitudes which Northrop Frye characterizes as marking a "garrison mentality."[7] Professor Frye and his followers have often written of the terror of vast, menacing natural forces which makes Canadians over-protective of the niceties of civilization — garrisoned against the wilderness, the "bush". The plot of *Bogle Corbet* reflects this garrison tension. Bogle Corbet, the middle-aged entrepreneur in charge of a group of "Paisley bodies " — weavers, carpenters and other tradesmen — exploits their terror of the storm, keeps them together in community work, pushes and pulls them into "civil reciprocity". The opposite of wild nature is the town — twice as dear to Galt and his persona in this wild ragged setting as Irvine or Kilmarnock or Greenock had been.

The founding of a new town is a deeply significant event, to be celebrated in fact and in fiction. In the third volume of *Bogle Corbet,* the founding of "Stockwell" provides whatever plot-line there is; indeed one should see the whole three volumes as moving through Bogle's life to that climactic event.

In analyzing this central scene, we can compare it to the other accounts of town-founding, in which Galt gradually added elements, touching up details, underlining the legendary nature of the event, and clarifying the ideals on which the town was founded.[8] For example,in an article in *Fraser's Magazine,* Galt recalls walking toward the site of the new town with Tiger Dunlop, lost, and without a compass, "like Babes in the Woods".[9] In a letter to D.M.Moir, Galt writes of the silence; thousands of pigeons and a doe with her fawn watched the quiet ceremony of cutting down the first tree at Guelph.[10] The *Autobiography* focuses also on the silence of the woods, that echoed to the sound of the axe "as the sigh of the solemn genius of the wilderness departing forever" (II, 59). In *Bogle Corbet,* the tonalities are different. At the founding of Stockwell, a distant noise is heard in the forest, "hoarse, dreadful, and mighty"; the stormy mood in nature acts to drive the settlers together, and to make them accept Corbet's view of the necessity of cooperative enterprise, the building of a common shelter, to precede the raising of individual houses.

Interestingly, another set of details from the non-fictional accounts reappear in a founding scene in *Lawrie Todd.* Tiger Dunlop had been remembered in the *Autobiography* as draping himnself in a blanket, as kilt-cum-toga, and drinking whiskey in a toast to "the unbuilt metropolis of the New World." John McTaggart, in *Three years in Canada,* building on oral reports, has Dunlop dancing "like a red genius of the place."[11]. In *Annals of the Town of Guelph,* another witness is quoted as remembering that Dunlop laid a lady's fan on the stump of the tree to suggest a possible layout of the streets.[12] *In Lawrie Todd* these details coalesce: Bailie Waft and Lawrie Todd walk together lovingly, "like two Babes in the Woods",and together aim ceremonial blows at a great tree, "banishing the loneliness and silence of the woods forever"; a feast follows, and the eccentric Bailie snaps his fingers and sings, as Lawrie Todd dances a reel with him. The more celebratory tone in this version is a contrast with the rather gloomy and threatened moment of the founding of the Canadian "Stockwell".

Into the account of the founding of an American town, Galt aptly inserted colorful details of eccentric characters and energetic action. The Canadian version has a more ironic tone. The townsmen are small-minded, the sense of community is fragile. There is a colonial awareness that the real centre of life is far away: one older man says, "There's a wide difference, Sir, between the Gorbals and this wild country"; others are "ay threepin' of Glasgow".

In writing of "the half-dozen of houses called Stockwell" Galt is in fact working in two directions. He celebrates town life, even on so small and undistinguished a scale, as being better than "these wild and interminable woods". He brings to the founding of a city all his anti-romantic bias, and all his personal preference for protection against the elements. As Bogle Corbet says, "We see it is from towns in all countries that cultivation proceeds." (65).

But the scale *is* small, and the town far from satisfying those ideals of the city which Galt held so strongly. A new world city should be "an asylum for the exiles of society"; but Bogle Corbet is hard pressed to provide for Mrs. Paddock and her grandsons, or to find proper occupations for Captain Campbell of Dungowan or for the distinguished -looking Colonel Jocelyn. The city should be the centre of an economic complex; but Stockwell has no periphery to draw from, and the business story of launching enterprises such as the mill is one of strain and exhaustion rather than of exhilaration. Town life is an ideal toward which man should aspire , but the Canadian actuality seems fragmented, unpredictable, insecure — a random gathering at a tavern, a collectionof half-interested people turning out to hear an itinerant Methodist preacher, neighbours running to extinguish a brush-fire set by the hired boy — "Siccan an owre muckle a fire, Sammy!" — so much too much of natural disaster still impending!

In Scotland, Galt could write "Annals of a parish": stories of a place where people are linked by a common belief and form of worship, webbed into a social network with the minister and elders at a centre of prestige. In Canada, Galt faced an unfamiliar pluralism. In planning Guelph he laid the groundwork for at least three overlapping parishes — Roman Catholic, Anglican, and Presbyterian.

John Galt establishes an ironic tone,in dealing with "Stockwell", emphasizing the discrepancy between the ideal of civility and the actualities of a disorganized small town. In this tone he foreshadows the work of Stephen Leacock, of Duncan Campbell Scott, L.M.Montgomery and many other small-scale ironic realists in Canadian literature. "Mariposa", with its abortive efforts at grandeur, festivities, and economic development, is Stockwell updated. Alice Munro's stories about "Jubilee" re-establish the same tone, in small-town fictions of our own day.

Not only in tone, but also in form, Galt's *Bogle Corbet* provided a preview of a major line of Canadian writing. In his annals of town life in Scotland Galt had never developed very strong consequential plots. In Auldbiggings and Garnock, the interlocking of lives might well have justified the use of such devices as revelations of hidden identity, sudden acquisition of power or wealth, or the masked battery of ill-will against innocent youth. In practice, Galt generally left such plot manipulation to his great rival Walter Scott. Plot complications appear in Galt's Scottish stories as minor elelments; his stories are held together more by the sense of slowly-developing political, theological, or economic change than by plot twists. In the Canadian novel, only vestiges of the romance plot remain, and they obtrude as excrescences in the story. (The Colonel Jocelyn — Captain Campbell — Mrs. Paddock connection is a characteristically awkward contrivance.)

But in *Bogle Corbet* no strong unifying societal development appears, in lieu of a romance plot — nothing like the slow unfolding of community feeling in Dalmailing, or Gudetown, or Garnock. The chapters of *Bogle Corbet* succeed each other as a random sequence of scenes. Chapter titles suggest the inconsequence: "Emigrants", "Miscellanies", "Evasions","Visitors", "Experiments": sharp vignettes catching single motifs in the life of the new town,in no particular order of intensity. The inconsequential form seems to countervail the highly individualistic theology of Galt's characters — the Calvinistic sense of the importance of the individual soul, self-examining, self-sufficient as moral judge. The form then adds to the ironies : its atomizing, unfused structure seems to counter the mores of diligence, economy, and self-discipline.

This form, the sequence of sketches, turned out to be very well suited to Canadian materials, long after Galt had departed and Guelph had gone its inconsequential way in development, depression, prosperity, recession. T.C. Haliburton's *The Clockmaker, or The sayings and doings of Sam Slick of Slickville* (1836) reports a haphazard collection of events — sayings and doings of a small Nova Scotia community , mostly Scots in origin, barely stirred by the energetic and eccentric presence of the Yankee salesman Sam. Mrs. Moodie's *Roughing it in the bush* (1852) sets its sketches near Peterborough, east of Toronto; the form is again a series rather than an integrated line of story. As the nineteenth century unfolded, collections of stories came from Quebec, in Duncan Campbell Scott's *In the Village of Viger (1896)* and Gilbert Parker's *The Lane that had no turning* (1900).[13] Montgomery moved the setting for comparable sketches to Prince Edward Island in *Anne of Avonlea* (1915); F.P. Grove set his vignettes in the West, in *Over Prairie Trails* (1922); Emily Carr took the form all the way to the West Coast in *The House of All Sorts* (1944). Galt's rough form seemed to fit easily into stories of a rough land, a terrain of moraines and drumlins and eskers,shoreline and prairie and Rockies. In social terms, the form seemed also appropriate for the disunified unharmonious small-town life of Canadian communities.

Galt had studied the specifics of town development in Scotland and England; in what seemed to him his own greatest achievement he had established a new town in Guelph, set sociably and rationally against the wilderness. He had planned a city that would be unified, beautiful. Hardly had he left Guelph when a new, less unified plan superseded his. A block was built across the fan-shaped design and the public space was virtually destroyed. Practical townsmen had responded firmly — against the dream. As in so many small Canadian towns, divisiveness grew in Guelph. Businesses competed, ethnic groups became set against each other, churches perpetuated differences in separate schools. But by that time Galt had left Guelph. Like the last of the lairds, like the young Pringles, like Anne, Dell, and Stephen Leacock, Galt had moved away from the small town, and gone (though not in triumph) to the metropolis.

John Galt, the founder of Guelph, had left behind him another foundation — an art form which was to become a privileged genre in Canadian literature, catching in its tough, ironic, honest way the best and the worst features of small town life.

NOTES

[1]*The Autobiography of John Galt,* 2 vols. (London: Cochrane and McCrone, 1833), I, 8.

[2]*Bogle Corbet, or the emigrants,* 3 vols. (London: Colburn and Bentley, 1831); 3 rd vol. rept., ed. Elizabeth Waterston (Toronto: McClelland and Stewart, 1977), pp. 160-163. Page citations in this essay will refer to the Toronto edition.

[3]*The Provost* (Edinburgh: Blackwood, 1822), ch. 24.

[4]*The Entail,* 3 vols. (Edinburgh: Blackwood, 1822), p. 322.

[5]*The Last of the Lairds* (Edinburgh: Blackwood, 1826), p. 101. I am indebted to Nick Whistler, who drew my attention to the recurrence of these frightening scenes.

[6]*Lawrie Todd, or the settlers* (London: Cochrane and McCrone, 1830), ch. 10.

[7]Northrop Frye, "Conclusion", in *Literary History of Canada,* ed. C.F. Klinck (Toronto: University of Toronto, 1965), p. 830.

[8]Nick Whistler, in "Truth and fiction: *The Autobiography of John Galt*" (unpublished M.A. thesis, University of Guelph, 1984), notes many variants of the account of the founding of Guelph, and speculates on their meanings.

[9]"Guelph in Upper Canada", *Fraser's Magazine* (November, 1830).

[10]Galt to Moir, April 30, 1827, Galt Papers, Public Archives of Canada.

[11]John McTaggart, *Three years in Canada* (London: Colburn), 1829, p. 204. 1877)

[12]C.A. Burrows, ed., *Annals of the town of Guelph* (Guelph: Herald, 1877)

[13]Ian Campbell traced a connection between some of the writers of this late Victorian period in Canada and the conventions of the Kailyard novel, in "Knowles of Galt", *Scottish Tradition,* 1982, pp. 163-176. Dr. Campbell and others have elsewhere suggested links between Galt and the Kailyard school.

Bogle Corbet and the Sentimental Romance

Martin Bowman

When John Galt published *Sir Andrew Wylie* and *The Entail* in 1822, more than half a century had elapsed since the first appearance of Henry Mackenzie's *The Man of Feeling*. Nevertheless, the cult of sensibility and the associated genre of the sentimental romance have a crucial influence on Galt's fiction. To date, Galt's use of these elements of eighteenth-century prose fiction has been either ignored — Carey Kaplan, for one, writes of "that absence of sentimentality which makes Galt's novels so different from most other popular Scottish novels of the period"[1] — or regretted. Such observations notwithstanding, the careful reader of Galt and of such a writer as Ann Radcliffe will inevitably see that Galt owes a considerable debt to the fictional models with which the writers of gothic and sentimental fiction provided him. Everywhere in his fiction, Galt struggles to develop and transform conventions drawn from his reading of sentimental romance.

Galt used the conventions of the sentimental romance continually, and almost always they created difficulties for him as he sought to portray society in a realistic manner in his theoretical histories. In particular, critics have observed the deleterious effect of sentimentalism in *Sir Andrew Wylie* and *The Entail,* two of Galt's most important books. Indeed *The Entail* has come to be regarded by some critics as Galt's masterpiece despite an almost universal regret that the book is spoiled by the intrusion of the sentimental romance into the realistic, even naturalistic, triumph of the book's tragedy. Similarly, the comic romance of *Sir Andre Wylie* has been harmed by what critics have tended to see as the bald imitation of an outworn tradition. Ultimately, we may want to affirm that these books are flawed in this way but examination will suggest that Galt was working quite consciously to integrate his material in a particular manner. It is not an entirely satisfactory approach to dismiss as mere padding the sentimental conventions wherever they appear. That suggests a cynicism which too much of Galt's achievement precludes. Even if the sentimental romance is used by Galt to enlarge his works to the required three-volume format, there would remain the question: why in these circumstances did he always resort to the same tradition?

Bogle Corbet, or the Emigrants, Galt's Canadian novel, shows more clearly than any other of his works the significance of the sentimental romance to his fiction. "A theoretic biography,"[2] the book is a fictional autobiography of an individual who describes himself as "a very ordinary man, distinguished, however, I must say, by a few adventures. . ." (I, 1-2). More important, *Bogle Corbet* is the study of a failure, a more energetic version of a little man like Thomas Duffle of *The Steam-Boat,* but as apt as the Glasgow cloth-merchant "to fall into an unaccountable mood of sadness. . ." (II, 187). Corbet must earn a living in business, but his melancholy temperament — he is clearly a descendant of the Man of Feeling — has rendered him totally unsuited to the exigencies of commercial life. *Bogle Corbet* has plenty of undigested sentimental material, but, as Elizabeth Waterston has observed, there is "a reductive spirit at work"[3] in the book which makes it a particularly interesting example of the tension between realism and romance in Galt's fiction. The prototype for this book is certainly *The Steam-Boat* with its combination of narrative and interpolated tales, most of which are drawn from the gothic-sentimental tradition. In the case of *Bogle Corbet,* however, the seams between the realistic framework and the romance adventures are less visible. Here the episodes are for the most part integrated into the life story of the protagonist. There is only one interpolated tale of little relevance to the central theme. Jennie Aberdein has observed that it "runs the gamut of Galt's various styles"[4]; nevertheless, she accepts Galt's claim that the book is didactic. *Bogle Corbet,* Galt wrote:

> was intended by me to be a guide book, particularly in the third volume, and I have in all my works, kept the instructive principle more or less in view. . . I considered the novel as a vehicle, parables, in which the moral was more valuable than the incidents were impressive.[5]

To see how far Galt wandered from his declared aim, consider the following passage from the first volume of the novel. Anella, Bogle's first wife, is very much the sentimental heroine. The fact that Bogle and she have married for love makes her early death as inevitable as it is conventional.

> Anella was several months advanced in the interesting state in which all good ladies wish to be who love their lords, and it was with an exquisitely painful reluctance that I left her. I wish not, however, to indulge my feelings here. The consequences that ensued supply materials for a sad tale, but I shall try to speak with cheerfulness, and to tell my story as the events came to pass. — Vain attempt! it is not in my power; my paper is blistered with the tears of remembrance, and I must pause (I, 185).

Such a passage demonstrates Galt's use of sentimentalism at its most derivative. Bogle is here situated in the classic position of the hero of sensibility. The only gesture towards realism is Bogle's declared attempt to restrain the indulgence of his feelings. Yet Bogle, considered in terms of the book as a whole, is not a sentimental hero but rather an example of the little man, the modern anti-hero — Waterston has identified him as "the first of a long line of Canadian anti-heroes"[6] — which we see emerging first in the character of Thomas Duffle. Such figures appear throughout Galt's best work, nowhere more powerfully than in the long-neglected novella, "The Betheral," which Galt published in his *Literary Life, and Miscellanies.*

The preface to *Bogle Corbet* gives a much more accurate impression of the book which follows than Galt's declarations in his autobiographical writings. "The object of this work has been to give expression to the probable feelings of a character upon whom the commercial circumstances of the age have had their natural effect, and to show what a person of ordinarily genteel habits has really to expect in emigrating to Canada" (I, iii). In Galt's study of an ordinary man, ill-suited to the demands of commercial life, the excesses of the cult of sensibility must be hidden. Bogle suffers because of his feelings which he cannot afford to show to the world; he must mask his sensibility from the rough-and-tumble business world where he earns his bread. At the outset of the novel he explains his emotions:

> Strange! that I should be thus so sentimental — I, who have so often been deemed but indifferently furnished with the gentler feelings. But so I fancy it is with most men; the outward gladness and the inward grief are often in harsh discord with one another. They have through life been so with me — and with others. — Alas! man is less a hypocrite than Fortune; she it is that makes us wear a mask — a smiling countenance with a weeping heart. . .(I, 5).

We have a picture from the very beginning of a man whose feelings are not for public exhibition, a man who realizes that to survive in the modern world he must betray his own nature. Bogle is acutely aware that he is a social misfit. At the end of the book, he remains in the self-sought isolation which his failure has driven him to find.

Bogle begins his career "as an operative in the workshop of Mr. Aird" (I, 35) where his "whole imagination was filled with shuttles and looms" (I, 36). The French Revolution, however, intervenes: "Commerce, in consequence, was suddenly driven back — much mercantile distress ensued" (I, 61). Bogle, Galt makes it clear, is not just a victim of his sensibility but, as a worker, suffers the effects of economic recession. He is only one small figure in the complicated, interconnected machinery of international economics. His failure sends him to London where, like Galt himself and so many of his protagonists, a "feeling of loneliness took possession" (I, 122) of him.[7] The city is an alien environment to Bogle, who delights in "the wild, the beautiful, and the grand of Nature. . ." (I, 123-124).

Up to this point, Galt has employed the conventions of sensibility fiction to develop the character of his unhappy realistic anti-hero. Corbet himself is fully aware of his problem. He is a superstitious man who believes in the occult linking of personalities. He sees in the figure of Eric Pullicate, whose success seems to increase proportionally to Bogle's failure, his own demon of destiny. This belief in doubles is, of course, found throughout gothic-sentimental fiction; in *Bogle Corbet,* however, Galt succeeds in integrating the convention into his realism. The reader is not required for a second to believe that "a preordained arrangement inscrutably exists between the fortunes of individuals who have no apparent connexion" (I, 151). Bogle sees himself as a victim of forces he cannot help — specifically his own feelings and the economic conditions of his time — and a mystical interpretation of reality helps him cope with his failure. Bogle himself is self-conscious about the belief: "Unaccountable fancies often molest the most prosaic minds" (I, 151). It is not so much that Pullicate is mystically linked to Corbet as that he represents all that Corbet recognizes as lacking in himself:

> I am persuaded, from the natural talent of the man, that he soon perceived the inherent commercial defects, not only obvious in my partner, but in myself. This is a humiliating acknowledgement, but unless it is frankly confessed, and freely explained, this work will neither produce the effect intended, nor be easily understood. . . . Eric Pullicate could not. . .avoid observing that all the inclinations of my character were averse to trade. His necessary constant attendance in the warehouse must have disclosed to him, before I left for London, that I was, to a most unfitting degree, prone to the indulgence of a meditative disposition, fantastical notions, and other follies of thought which, though they resemble philosophy, are in reality but the froth of the mind (I, 148-49).

This passage is immensely important to an understanding of Galt's purpose in *Bogle Corbet.* The book is a study of a mediocre man who frankly recognizes his limitations. Galt's interest here is entirely focused on the psychology of his ordinary protagonist who suffers all the ill effects of a melancholic disposition. The power of the book, when read in this light, lies in the fact that the failure tells his story in his own terms.

It cannot be surprising that this little man will shape his story to the conventions of the literature he has read. Bogle recognizes his excess of feeling in the heroes of sensibility; he says that he "imbibed a more general taste for reading, without acquiring a particular bias for any subject" (II, 56). He is from an early point self-conscious about himself as an author: "Indeed, it cannot be said that I very strictly confine myself to any regular story. The course of my biography is like the character of my life, somewhat desultory. . . I ever felt that I was out of my road" (I, 127). Like Balwhidder, Pawkie, Duffle, and Gilhaize before him, Corbet, as a first-person narrator, is actually writing his own account of his life. As the second Mrs. Corbet says near the end of the book: "Bogle Corbet there is busy. . .writing his life. . .he never met with a right novel-like adventure in all his days — what he read to me of it, is as common as an old newspaper. I wonder what some people think of themselves, when they expect others to read paternosters about their whims and nothings" (III, 283-84;.W, 189). The unoriginal mind of poor Bogle Corbet could not be expected to produce anything other than a largely derivative book. Because he sees himself as a kind of failed Man of Feeling, surely it is inevitable that he will couch his story in the terms he has. Galt, at least in this instance, has a structure and a character which legitimize his use of the conventions of the sentimental romance.

Bogle himself is aware of the lack of romance in his own life. Having married for love the first time, he chooses his second wife for practical reasons. His lack of business acumen, however, leads him to choose Urseline Ascomy, whose father is on the verge of ruin. In this way, Galt further develops the predicament of this ordinary man of feeling who fails even when he tries to be practical. At the time of his second marriage, he writes that "the romance of life was then becoming a little flat and stale with. . . . I honestly told |Urseline|, when I solicited the favour of paying my addresses, that we had both too many nicks in our horns to be pastoral in our love, without running the risk of being foolish" (II, 64-65). This marriage to a woman he does not love increases ". . . that disposition to evade society which has since become a second nature to |him| . . ." (II, 81). His failure in business he recognizes as unremarkable. Bogle is only one of many who go under; with the diminution of what little romance he had in his life, he feels he has become a less interesting individual: "The reader will however, I fear, be tired of these frequent allusions to the state of my commercial connexions. . . . He will see around him, by the altered condition of many, a sufficient illustration of my inevitable fate as participating in the fortunes of the kingdom" (II, 103-04). Bogle recognizes that he is not free; he sees himself like many others as a cog in the broken wheel of society. Galt places Corbet clearly in the context of contemporary society but does not idealize the figure of the helpless victim caught in forces beyond his control. The figure which Galt presents is more complicated than that; the reasons for Corbet's failure are shown to emerge from the interaction of social and personal elements.

As his penury increases, Corbet undertakes his "project of seeking refuge in the woods of America" (II, 170).

> Alike the victim of the times, of pecuniary accidents, and of family grievances, no prospect of happier fortune could be discovered, and hope for myself and my offspring existed only in a foreign land. In a word, I felt the strong hand of Fate pushing me on to emigrate; and I am the more anxious that this should be manifest, as some who have pretended to be interested in my proceeding have insinuated that, not necessity, but caprice and fancy instigated a determination in which so much hardship must be encountered, and all the enjoyments of friendly intercourse foregone (II, 173-74).

By this point in the story, Bogle's growing sense of victimization turns into paranoia. He no longer acknowledges a personal liability as a factor in his failure but blames the times, bad luck, and a nagging wife for the impossible situation which has developed. Further, he is sensitive to criticism of his reasons for emigration. Not his are any grandiose romantic schemes of discovery. Bogle emigrates to escape a dull, flat life out of which all the romance has gone.

At this point, Elizabeth Waterston's edition takes up the story of Bogle Corbet and, in this Canadian section, Galt consciously compares the ordinariness of life as Corbet finds it with his youthful expectations of romance. The failure of romance comes to symbolize the disappointed expectations of Galt's Canadian anti-hero himself. As Waterston observes:

> Religious fervor is reduced to disputes between sects. . . .The subplot, the story of old Mrs. Paddock and her family, hinges on the fact of bastardy, but that fact is not seen as a romantic bar sinister, but as a bothersome blight on the social expectations of the young boys.
>
> Bogle Corbet's story conveys also the sense of crisis, of tension, not by a melodramatic surface story, but by its acidly real picture of life in the raw little town of 1826.9

Bogle recognizes that in Canada he is in a new world requiring him to adjust his expectations. He is depressed by the lack of romance in the countryside which is "solitary, and, to say the truth, . . . to the emigrant a little saddening. It lacks the social cheerfulness of villages; . . . the gorgeous castle, the manorial hall, and the mouldering monastic piles of the olden time, which makes the landscape of England, in the variety of its imagery, so like the associations of the English mind (II, 302; W, 145). Later, however, he comes to appreciate the beauty of the place despite its lack of conventional picturesque: "The scene, without being mountainous, was cliffy and sylvan, wanting only ruins to be romantic. Few passages, if I may use the expression, in all Old England are so beautiful" (III, 217; W, 157).

There follows a brilliant scene concerning a visit to Niagara Falls which allows Galt to play off the dominant modes of the book one against the other. Niagara Falls, as we see in the reaction of a romantic young tourist, provides

> ". . . a stupendous scene. . . ."
>
> "The sublime of energy! — till this sight is seen, we can form no just conception of the power that may be in Nature. The rage of the ocean, with its countless waves, is but a passion in detail. This is the immense of simplicity; could we stand on the outside of a planet's orbit, and see the vast globe rolling along, at the velocity of thousands of miles an hour, it would not furnish a livelier visible image of Omnipotence!" (III, 234-35; W, 165-66).

This kind of over-reaction is put in perspective by Mrs. Corbet. Bogle wants to see the Falls but she desists: "'Go, Bogle, and be pacified; but of all the waterfalls that I have seen, the best is from the tea-kettle into the tea-pot: — by the time you come back I shall have an excellent cup ready for you'" (III, 225; W, 161). Bogle, of course, is likely to share the reactions of the "tall, meagre young man, of a pale, parson-like physiognomy," (III, 231; W, 164) but has come to realize that "there was more of a simple nature in Mrs. Corbet's feelings at the Falls than in those of many of the other visitors, were we to judge by their far-fetched and inflated phraseology" (III, 230; W, 163). Galt distinguishes here between the artificial diction of the cult of feeling and the genuine feeling, which is an important element in his characterization of the Corbets. Bogle seems to have come to the conclusion that reality is more interesting when notions of romance are not foisted upon it. Mrs. Corbet's inviting cup of tea suggests that the marriage, despite its lack of romance, has something to recommend it.

The reduction in Bogle's sentimental responses parallels the change in Bogle himself as he grows older, accepts his lot, and realizes that romance has little to do with reality. This transformation is emphasized in the use Galt makes in the Canadian section of the novel of the conventional romance subplot concerning Mrs. Paddock; she has left the old country because of the shame of her daughter's illegitimate children. The details of the subplot are convoluted and uninteresting, but eventually Jocelyn, a man with a mysterious past, turns up. While he is inextricably bound up with the story of Mrs. Paddock, he turns out to be not a lost lover nor a husband but her brother-in-law. Corbet's own life, despite his propensities for romance, entirely lacks the coincidences and revelations of the sentimental melodrama. Jocelyn tells his story to Mrs. Corbet who responds irrelevantly, "'Who ever thought I would be heroine, and live in a midnight turret in America?'" (III, 282; W, 188). The focus of interest is deflected here from the tired romance. Much more lively at this stage is the interaction of Bogle and Urseline, who have usurped the position of the romance hero and heroine. The final joke occurs when Jocelyn returns to London carrying Bogle's manuscript with him. The hero of romance is reduced to an errand boy for the realistic Canadian anti-hero. At the end of the book, Bogle has retired in self-imposed isolation. Interested in the beauties of nature, this anti-hero of sensibility has taken up the hobby of indoor gardening: "Our parlour is often filled with the vapour, fume, and fragrance, of these vegetable investigations; and a pastime having an object, has tended to diminish the tediousness of that time to which the epithet of precious ought to be applied" (III, 300-01; W, 197). The final picture then is of a Man of Feeling utterly transformed into an ordinary little man making do with the remainder of an undistinguished life.

There are many lapses in *Bogle Corbet* but, of all Galt's fiction, it constitutes the most important achivement in adapting the conventions of the sentimental romance to the requirements of his realism. Elsewhere, Galt either imitated or parodied the conventions with varying degrees of success. When, for example, he succeeded in employing parody in the service of his characterization, he achieved, in *The Ayrshire Legatees,* a measurable effect. Elsewhere parody and imitation were employed in the same book and the resultant contradiction either seriously interfered with Galt's vision in such a major work as *The Entail* or utterly destroyed it in such hackwork as *Stanley Buxton.* In these terms, it seems to me that *Bogle Corbet* represents an important achievement in Galt's struggle with the conventions of his fiction-writing predecessors. The parody of such conventions depends on exaggeration for its effect whereas in this book, as in the example of the disclosure of Jocelyn's secret, Galt works in the opposite direction. To begin with, Bogle details the events of his early life very much in terms which imitate the sentimental romance. As he grows older, however, his style moderates as he comes to accept that his life is no romance. This is particularly true in the last section of the book where Galt includes a subplot based on the romance storyline which flawed such books as *Sir Andrew Wylie* and *The Entail.* In *Bogle Corbet,* the melodramatic plot serves to emphasize the importance of the virtually plotless story of Bogle and Urseline as they settle into their Canadian life and, through its awkwardness and lack of real interest, the reader appreciates the importance of Galt's realistic picture of ordinary and totally unsentimentalized people.

Bogle Corbet lacks the power of such a book as *The Entail.* Galt's field of interest is much narrower here than in the earlier work and inevitably the book is a lesser achievement. *Bogle Corbet* is important, however, because it shows that Galt was able to discover a way of successfully integrating the conventions of the sentimental romance into a book which is the antithesis of that mode. In the figure of Bogle Corbet, Galt created a protagonist who reflects the conflicting elements of his own imagination. Bogle may be a descendant of the Man of Feeling and other sentimental heroes, but he is, first and foremost, an ordinary individual specifically localized in time and place. Having glimpsed his own insignificance in the scheme of things, he survives at the end of the book, tending his plants in a retirement cottage. Galt's refusal to frame Bogle's life in a melodramatic plot recognizes the tremendous resonance of the quiet tragedy of a man who lives out his life trying to avoid the tedium of ordinary circumstances.

The conventions of sentimental fiction created real difficulties for Galt. He achieved tentative solutions to the problems elsewhere in his fiction, in *The Ayrshire Legatees* and *The Entail,* for example, but only in *Bogle Corbet* was he able to solve the problems of characterization and melodramatic plot which, as a sort of residuary legatee, he inherited from the practitioners of sentimental romance.

NOTES

[1]Carey H. Kaplan, "John Galt and the Scottish Novel," Diss. Univ. of Massachusets 1972, p. 75.

[2]John Galt, *Bogle Corbet: or, the Emigrants,* 3 vols. (London, 1831), I, iv. Elizabeth Waterston's edition, *Bogle Corbet* (Toronto: McClelland and Stewart, 1977), begins at a point in II, 229 of the first edition and reproduces Galt's text from there to the end of Volume III. In this paper, references to the novel account for both editions, references to the Waterston edition appearing with the abbreviation "W".

[3]Elizabeth Waterston, Introduction, *Bogle Corbet,* ed. Elizabeth Waterston (Toronto: McClelland and Stewart, 1977), p. 6.

[4]Jennie W. Aberdein, *John Galt* (London: Oxford Univ. Press, 1936), p. 172.

[5]John Galt, *The Autobiography of John Galt.* 2 vols. (London, 1833), II, 210.

[6]Waterston, p. 1.

[7]From the first, Galt felt somewhat alienated in London, a theme he often repeated in

his fiction: "On different occasions I have attempted to describe the feelings of a stranger when he first arrived in London, but all of them are mitigated compared with what I experienced" (*Autobiography,* I, 63). Among the characters to whom he refers are Thomas Duffle, Bogle Corbet, and the Pringles, father and son. A contrasting opinion is expressed in Galt's first published novel, *The Majolo: A Tale* 2 vols. (London, 1816): "'. . . although the magnificent picture which my ignorance had embodied with the smoke, was dispersed, the impression of the scene has never been effaced; and the first view of London will ever stand in my remembrance as a spectacle of the utmost sublimity. It had the effect of making me regard the town as invested with something at once tremendous and inexplicable. . .'" (II, 48-49).

[8]Waterston, pp. 6-7.

The Epistolary Novel and John Galt's *The Ayrshire Legatees*

Keith M. Costain

After Richardson had given classic status to the epistolary novel its popularity was such that between 1742 and 1785 it became the predominant type of prose fiction in England. The form declined after 1785 but it did not fall. Not only did it "give the letter to the novel as part of its natural impedimenta" but full-length epistolary novels continued to be written. G.F. Singer observed of the form in 1933 that it "has taken its place for almost a century and a half now as a normal form of literature, to be resorted to by the occasional author from time to time."[1] It still shows vital signs.[2]

In a book on the Familiar Letter in Russia William Mills Todd remarks that:

> writers do not merely copy the schema a genre sets before them but make a personal relationship to it a part of their creative fusion of material and form, adapting, rejecting, or changing the schema that they share with the experienced reader.[3]

Jane Austen was unable to establish a satisfactory "personal relationship" with the schema of the epistolary novel and turned to "the more economical method of direct narrative."[4] John Galt, on the other hand, achieved the "economy" his contemporary sought without abandoning the letter form. In *The Ayrshire Legatees*, published serially in *Blackwood's Edinburgh Magazine* in 1820-21 and then revised and re-issued as a volume, he made a compromise with the form. Letters constitute the bulk of the novel but there are also passages of direct narrative which give the work a scope wider than letters alone would allow.[5] This essay will examine Galt's "personal relationship" with the schema of the epistolary novel, the "creative fusion of material and form" which he makes in this work in order to accomplish one of his principal aims in writing fiction, namely to engage in what he called "the metaphysical anatomy" of character, or what today we would call psychological analysis.[6]

II

The central theme of *The Ayrshire Legatees* is that of judgment the nature of which, and of the influences which affect it — especially the social and historical influences — can only be laid bare by an analysis of character in the context of a particular environment. Clear-sighted, sympathetic judgment is always desirable but it is a pressing personal necessity at times when the values which guide it are in conflict. This was the case in 1820, the year in which Galt both wrote and set the novel. In 1820 the long reign of George III came to an end and, for Galt, this marked a significant historical turning-point. When the king came to the throne British society was still largely agricultural but when he died the industrial system with its factories, its steam-engines, its urbanization, was producing a social reality unique in history. The communal values of the rural village were being challenged by the practitioners and the theorists of unregulated capitalism for whom self-interest was the prime legitimate motive in the market-place. At the same time the technological developments of the age were hailed as "improvements": as visible evidence of Man's progress.

As well as momentous economic changes there were great political changes in the reign of George III. At the beginning of his reign the revolutions in the American colonies and in France were yet to come; by the time of the King's death "public opinion" could no longer be ignored. Radicals and reactionaries were in open conflict on the long march that led, eventually, to the Reform Act of 1832 and beyond. Galt was very much aware of the gulf that separated the present in which he was writing from the political environment of his Georgian youth, as when he observes that:

> For statesmen to reason and to act now according to the maxims of their predecessors — that is, of those who were in power before the French Revolution, and who, by not discerning how much of a change in political dogmas was involved in the evolutions of that catastrophe, accelerated its devastations, would be to condemn the instruction of history, and to betray a total ignorance of the character and spirit of the age.[7]

History, then, had made a forceful appearance even among the lives of ordinary people, and had demonstrated that standards of judgment, like social institutions, are subject to change. Thus in *The Ayrshire Legatees* Galt's "metaphysical anatomy" is not only designed, after the manner of Fielding, to reveal what typifies the genus "Human Nature" but to show how character, and therefore judgment, is affected for good or ill by the "character and spirit of the age." This intention is made clear by the generation gap which separates the Pringles, the novel's protagonists. The values of the elder Pringles are in harmony with what Galt conceived to be the "spirit" of the agricultural society that existed early in the reign of George III; they are the values of the village, the values associated with community. Those of the younger Pringles have been influenced by the "spirit" of what Galt thought of as a less compassionate mercantile and industrial society; they are values associated with the city. Broadly speaking — for, as we shall see, there are exceptions to these generalizations — the judgment of the elder Pringles is affected by concern for others while that of their offspring is swayed by their preoccupation with themselves. The values of the two generations of Pringles come into conflict in their epistolary observations upon what they see on their journey to and during their prolonged stay in London to which they have come from the rural village of Garnock, in Ayrshire, in order to collect a legacy. The conflict is representative of that which Galt observed in society at large at the time he wrote the novel.

However much the moral qualitites of the Pringles may differ each in his own way brings a provincial perspective to bear upon life in London, the modern city *par excellence* in 1820. In doing so they illustrate the manner in which culture as well as history helps to shape character and to influence judgment. Galt takes this provincial perspective seriously for no matter how much comedy the Pringles' situation engenders they are not dismissed as country bumpkins come to town.[8]

The letter allowed Galt to create a natural and coherent union of theme, the character-analysis on which it depends, and form. When people write letters, in life and in literature, they are inclined to be judicial and when they are being judicial they reveal themselves to their readers, often unwittingly. This is especially likely to be the case when, as with the Pringles, the letter-writer is away from home, evaluating, for the benefit of those left behind, an unfamiliar environment at once frightening, exciting, and puzzling.

In spite of the sophistication and depth of his more direct analysis of a character such as Claud Walkinshaw in his later novel, *The Entail,* Galt generally chose to remain off-stage, ". . . to keep out of view every thing that might recall the separate existence of John Galt" as he explains in his *Literary Life.*[9] His characters, like those in a play, reveal themselves in the limelight and in *The Ayrshire Legatees* the epistolary form enabled them to do so.[10] Familiar letters are written conversation — to use Pope's phrase, "talking on paper,"[11] comparable to talking on stage — and permit an unmediated revelation of each character's capacity for effective moral and practical judgment. The letter form was congenial to a writer who was an avid theatre-goer, who eagerly read and wrote plays, and who had suffered what George Eliot in her essay on Heine calls "that chicken-pox of authorship, the production of a tragedy."

Further, the epistolary novel deals with change. It is concerned not with recounting a completed action but with individual responses to action unfolding, action the twists and turns of which provoke corresponding shifts and changes of attitude, opinion, mood, and tone on the part of the observing letter-writers. Since Galt depicts good judgment not as a rigidly fixed set of criteria but as an operation of the mind constantly affected by experience, especially the experience of change, of difference, and of error, then the considerable flexibility of the epistolary form proved aesthetically appropriate to his theme.

Galt, however, was a realist guided by probability[12] and had he simply taken the eighteenth-century epistolary novel as he found it some of its elements would have proven inimical to his point of view. His "personal relationship" with the schema of the epistolary form caused him to modify it in order to meet the standards of probability.

Scott points out some of the weaknessess of the epistolary form as it developed in the eighteenth-century when it is judged by such standards. He writes:

> In order that all my be written, which must be known for the purpose of the narrative, characters must frequently write, when it would be more natural for them to be acting — must frequently write what it is not natural to write at all — and must at all times write a good deal oftener, and a great deal more, than one would think human life had time for.[13]

Galt avoids such departures from probability as Scott mentions by having the Pringles write letters that create the impression of an actual correspondence. The letters are of credible length: they don't run into journals or treatises as in eighteenth-century epistolary fiction they tend to do. In fact Galt satirizes this tendency when Rachel, the Pringles' daughter, writes to her correspondent in Garnock to say that the "interruptions" to her "observations" occasioned by sea-sickness on the stormy voyage to London from Leith "made me destroy my journal."[14]

The Pringles are not given to exhaustive self-analysis though they do reflect upon their experience. They have no option but brevity when commenting upon the people and events that have interested them most for they go out and about, writing when they have time. They are not, like a Richardsonian heroine, confined pen in hand vainly attempting to capture and set down the flying moments. There is a hint of *Shamela* in Galt's dig at Richardson's "to the moment" formula when Rachel is busily engaged in describing her London landlady (neither a Mrs. Jewkes nor a Mrs. Sinclair). Rachel breaks off with a hasty "But I am interrupted" as if she were Pamela with Mr. B-- at the door or Clarissa with Lovelace at the keyhole. The interruption, in fact, is caused by no more alarming a person than a "man of business" come to see her father about the legacy.

The difficulties with probability manifested in eighteenth-century epistolary fiction arise, in part, because like any other type of fiction this must tell a story and yet there is no narrator to perform this function. The major characters are letter-writers engaged in what we are asked to accept as a private correspondence. They may, as we all do, include snatches of narrative in their letters but they do not see their lives as a narrator would see them — as elements of a literary construct — unless, as with Clarissa, the author turns his protagonist into a surrogate novelist. All too often, in the absence of a narrator, the epistolary novel obliges characters to play incompatible roles as perhaps Jane Austen realized when she re-drafted the early versions of what were to be *Pride and Prejudice* and *Sense and Sensibility.* As characters they write with limited, uncertain knowledge both of themselves and of present events yet, perforce, they must be narrators too, helping to unfold a story with a shape and a coherence that only retrospect and the distance logically unavailable to the letter-writer can give it.

Galt's Pringles are not surrogate novelists. They write their letters unaware to the end that they are providing the raw material for a story. Galt takes the "editor," who appears in prefaces to many eighteenth-century novels to attack Romance and insist upon the historical veracity of the story to follow, and mingles his editorial function with that of unobtrusive narrator. Thus it is the "editor's" selection of the Pringles' letters, his suggestive, ironic juxtaposition of them, and his own passages of narrative (which vary from a few lines to all of the final chapter) that mould a story of wider import than any of the letter-writers, with their necessarily limited points of view, could tell.

Galt's "editor," like the "editor" of *Sartor Resartus*, is "limited" to commenting upon his primary texts, the letters. Like Carlyle and many another writer Galt found the editorial mask dramatically useful because it deflects attention from the author while, behind the mask, he intimates how his characters and the events with which he associates them are to be comprehended. In their letters the characters reveal themselves directly but through his "editor," indirectly, Galt establishes a context in relation to which their experience gains in thematic significance.

In order to avoid any hint of omniscience, which would be inconsistent with the dramatic nature of *The Ayrshire Legatees*, the "editor" is not only "limited" to a brief, if telling, commentary but he is set among the characters in that he is a member of the community in which the Pringles have led their lives. He collects their letters, he says, after hearing some of them read aloud at "a great tea-drinking held in the Kirkgate of Irvine at the house of Miss Mally Glencairn" (II, 104). He writes about the Pringles as actual people of his acquaintance through to the last chapter in which he observes, with the immediacy of the letter-writers themselves, that "Mrs. Pringle is at present actively preparing to remove from the manse"; that Andrew Pringle's correspondent, Mrs. Snodgrass, "was last week declared helper and successor to the doctor"; and that his marriage to Isabella, Rachel Pringle's correspondent, "will take place with all convenient expedition (II, 279). The "editor's" intimacy with the people of whom he writes; his first-hand knowledge of their milieu; and also the irony, available to him as an acute, impartial observer, by means of which he can put them into perspective, all give him authority as both sympathetic portrait-artist and critic.

In keeping with the dramatic mode of *The Ayrshire Legatees* the "editor's" criticism is indirect for the most part. The narrative passages are largely orchestrations by the "editor" of the voices of the Pringles' friends commenting critically upon each letter as it arrives and is read aloud. The "editor" conducts a dramatic "chorus" which provides suggestions as to how the respective letters are to be interpreted. He draws attention, ironically, to his dramatic model when toward the end of the novel he writes: "Thus were all the correspondents of the Pringles assembled by the merest chance, like the *dramatis personae* at the end of a play" (II, 250).

As each letter from the Pringles arrives their acquaintance "review" it like the reviewers who worked for journals such as that in which this novel was first published, though they do so "in their way" (II, 83). These "commentators" on each "epistle" (II, 224) give the reader direct access to the provincial culture which has helped form the Pringles and has provided some of the important criteria by which they assess London. The "editor's" record of the reception of the Pringles' letters by a representative group of provincial people establishes a cultural context for them and thus a way of understanding the family and its experiences.

The elements of the provincial culture which the members of the "chorus" express include especially a practicality of mind, a down-to-earth Scottish common sense that causes the "commentators" unanimously to reject such postures, illusions, fancies, and affectations as new wealth and the London environment encourage in all but Mrs. Pringle. For that reason her letters are the most popular and the least criticized. The hyperbole of her children's letters, on the other hand, is regularly pricked by simple judgments delivered in the vernacular. After Becky Glibbans has listened to a letter read aloud in which Rachel coyly sings her own praises she remarks "Rachel had aye a gude roose of hersel'" (II, 237), and her mother dismisses Andrew Pringle's account of the funeral of George III as "a peesemeal of clishmaclavers." Her rhetorical question, inspired by Andrew, applies also to his sister, as we shall see. She asks, in her odd idiom, "What is sensibility without judgment. . . but a thrashing in the water and a raising of bells?" (II, 139).

The "chorus" does not always speak with one voice, however, for, as the "editor" remarks, "It is really surprising how differently the same thing affects different people" (II, 118). Over particular letters there is, therefore, "a considerable diversity of opinion" (II, 224). This "diversity" in *The Ayrshire Legatees* arises basically from the fact that some members of the Garnock-Irvine community take a more parochial view of the world than others. Those who are narrow-minded are shackled by local tradition and custom while others, who are more tolerant, more open-minded, seem to have responded to the liberating influence of natural beauty in their pastorally-depicted environs.[15] They respond with good-humoured tolerance to a "freshness" which "causes the spirits to sympathise with the universal cheerfulness of all nature" (II, 275).

The benevolent parish elder, Mr. Daff, is of the latter kind as is Mr. Snodgrass, "the gentle priest" (II, 177) whom Dr. Pringle has left in charge of his parish during his absence and who eventually succeeds him as Minister of Garnock. Neither Mr. Daff nor Mr. Snodgrass is tied to attitudes that are inherited and prejudiced and thus they come into conflict with two people especially whom the "editor" styles "the rigidly righteous Mr. Craig" (II, 132) and "the polemical Deborah of the Relief Kirk," Mrs. Glibbans (II, 152-3). The outlook of these two is shaped by their Presbyterian "orthodoxy," a cultural expression of their spiritual pride. When the Pringles lean toward the parochial narrowness of "orthodoxy" they are exposed through irony to the reader's criticism but when they incline to the fairmindedness of Mr. Snodgrass they show themselves worthy of praise. Mr. Snodgrass insists upon a sensible cultural relativity, informing his newly-acquired parishioners that "it is impossible to judge correctly of strangers by measuring them according to our own notions of propriety" (II, 225). The degree to which the Pringles absorb this lesson marks the extent to which their judgment is improved by their London adventure.

The Ayrshire Legatees has, then, three basic formal elements: the letters, the "chorus" of recipients, and the "editor" who relates the one to the other. Now that each of these elements has been abstractly identified and the functions of each discussed it is important to show how in the novel they work together dynamically to explore character and theme.

III

Dr. Pringle, Minister of the Parish of Garnock and the central character of *The Ayrshire Legatees,* exemplifies, like the pastoral landscape surrounding his village, the value which Galt thought most conducive to good moral judgment, the value of benevolence. The "editor" describes the Minister as the very embodiment of amiability for he is:

> Of that easy sort of feather-bed corpulency of form that betokens good nature... [having] none of that smooth, red, well-filled protuberancy, which indicates a choleric humour and a testy temper (II, 276).

The Minister's benevolent moral disposition is stimulated by his environment for he lives in close daily contact with natural beauty, his pastoral duties constantly call upon him to care for others, and his charity is unfailing. When he changes his environment on his visit to London, however, without the incitement of these stimuli he briefly succumbs to an ego-centricity that is represented in the novel as a characteristic fostered by modern city life, and this impairs his judgment.

Dr. Pringle's letters show that the more he becomes emotionally and psychologically distant from Garnock the cloudier grows his moral judgment, though it is some time before he realizes it. He leaves his parish in the charge of the admirable Mr. Snodgrass and his early letters to Mr. Micklewham, "Schoolmaster and Session-clerk of Garnock," indicate his continuing solicitude for the poor he has left behind. As soon as his legacy is secured he sends money back to Garnock to help the needy accompanied by instructions to Mr. Micklewham as to its disbursement. The precise detail of these instructions shows how, after a relatively recent arrival in the Capital, the Minister has both the needs and the character of the people he wants to help uppermost in his mind. He is especially sensitive to their attitudes about money. He displays a tolerant relativity of moral disposition when he tells his Session-clerk "You will give to auld Mizy Eccles ten shillings. She's a careful creature, and it will go as far with her thrift as twenty will do with Effy Hopkirk. So you will give

Effy twenty" (II, 110). Another parishioner's social rank must be taken into account for the offer of "charity" will offend her pride. Mr. Micklewham, therefore, must use diplomacy when offering money to Miss Betty Peerie for:

> Being a gentlewoman by both blood and education, she's a very slimmer affair to handle in a doing of this kind. But I am persuaded she's in as great necessity as many that seem far poorer, especially since the muslin flowering has gone down. Her bits of brats are sairly worn, though she keeps out an apparition of gentility (II, 111).

The tolerance and humanity of these directions are evident also when Dr. Pringle is obliged to consider the moral welfare of his parishioners. He does not condone moral laxity but he does understand and sympathise with human weakness so that he is incapable of the hypocritical zeal in moral judgment of either Mr. Craig or Mrs. Glibbans, who think only in terms of punishment for wrongdoing. When the Minister learns that Meg Milliken has had an illegitimate child by one Tam Glen (both members of his flock) he writes to Mr. Micklewham to say that the elders of his church — Mr. Craig in particular — are "no to be overly hard on that poor donsie thing." The Minister has no high regard for Meg, whom he describes as "something of a tawpie," but he tells his Session-clerk "You need no diminish her to Tam." He advises that Tam be persuaded to "own Meg for his wife" (II, 82).

Dr. Pringle's sympathetic counsel proves effective for in a later communication he expresses his pleasure at "the repentance of Tam Glen," who indeed married Meg. He also makes plain his irritation with Mr. Craig whose attempt to prevent the baptism of the illegitimately-conceived child was circumvented by Mr. Daff, his fellow-elder, and by Mr. Snodgrass. Mr. Craig professes himself deeply disturbed by the "carnality" of "his day and generation" (II, 133) but eventually finds himself in Tam Glen's situation, having impregnated then hastily married his own housekeeper. The Minister, however, does not rush to condemn him. Instead he writes to wish Mr. Craig "much joy and felicity," adding that this severe elder "should be milder in the future on the thoughtlessness of youth and headstrong passions" (II, 190). Had Mr. Daff been the moral truant, the Minister remarks in the same letter, Mr. Craig "would have sifted with a sharp eye how he came to be married in December, and without bridal and banquet" (II, 191).

Dr. Pringle mildly appreciates the irony of Mr. Craig's predicament but he is destined to be mortified by the irony to which, in his new environment, his own lapses of moral judgment give rise. The longer the Minister remains in London away from the milieu that nourishes his benevolent moral disposition the more he is inclined to act out of vanity and allow himself to be distracted from his pastoral obligations.

In Garnock Dr. Pringle is a person of consequence. He takes his social prominence for granted, as is evident when he describes his entry into London as though it were an entry to a greater Garnock. He writes that he became anxious about his seat on top of a coach, confiding naively to Mr. Micklewham that "I began to be ashamed of the sin of high places and would gladly have got into the inside of the coach, for fear of anybody knowing me." No-one, he innocently observes, "took the least notice of my situation" (II 91). Suddenly, the minister has become anonymous and he is not comfortable with anonymity. Thus, once he has obtained his legacy and lived for a while in the city he responds to the flattery of "the Saints," the group of evangelical philanthropists inspired by William Wilberforce.[16] They have designs upon the Minister's money and his time in pursuit of their charitable schemes toward which Dr. Pringle's benevolence naturally inclines him. "The Saints," however, provide Dr. Pringle with an opportunity to be noticed, to cut a figure on the London stage. He fills his days with Bible society meetings, missionary meetings, both listening to and preaching sermons. He acquires a very high opinion of his own talents and, as his wife worriedly comments in a letter of her own, acts "like an enchantit person" (II, 185). She is appalled that he has come to believe that "his candle has been hidden under a bushel at Garnock more than thirty years" (II, 187) but takes some small comfort from the fact that "he's happy in his delooshon" (II, 187). Thus does Dr. Pringle indeed become guilty of "the sin of high places." If benevolence is to guide the moral judgment effectively there can be no serious admixture of egoism.

Human frailty is not confined to the likes of Tam Glen or Mr. Craig for, ironically, the Minister's own experience reminds him that "the longer we live in this world, and the farther we go, and the better we know ourselves, the less reason have we to think slightingly of our neighbours" (II, 191). He is awakened to reality and to clearer moral judgment through the humiliation his vanity brings upon him. In a letter to his Session-clerk he describes how he preached a sermon in a London church very much to his own satisfaction only to find that he had sent his auditors to sleep. This fiasco causes him, he tells Mr. Micklewham, to withdraw "from trafficking so much as I did in the missionary ploys" in vogue in the metropolis for, he continues, it "will be better for my own people, as I will keep for them what I was giving to the unknown" (II, 230). Having been recalled to his proper obligations the Minister confesses that he has forgotten the particular needs of his parishioners of which, when he first came to London, he was so well apprised. He asks Mr. Micklewham to distribute money he has sent "amongst the poorest of the parish, according to the best of your discretion, my long absence having taken from me the power of judgment in a matter of this sort" (II, 261).

It is ironic that in the face of temptation a basically charitable, morally perceptive man should allow his vanity to run away with him but it is doubly ironic that he should clearly recognize this process in his son while remaining blind to it in himself. Andrew Pringle spends the family's new money even more extravagantly than his father in order to appear a "gentleman" to his new London acquaintance. Dr. Pringle wisely decides to let Andrew have his "fling," writing to his Session-clerk to say that "we will be obliged to let him take the length of his tether for a while." He adds, however, that his son will not be "altogether without a curb neither" (II, 163) and he applies the "curb" when Andrew proposes to buy a seat in the unreformed House of Commons. The Doctor's objections to Andrew's proposal are sound; he writes to Mr. Micklewham that his son:

> Is not yet come to years of discretion enough to sit in council, and, moreover, he has not been tried; and no man, till he has out of doors shown something of what he is, should be entitled to power and honour within (II, 164).

The irony of these objections lies in the fact that they are made by a man who has "come to years of discretion" yet at the time he makes them suffers under the delusion that he could become a great metropolitan preacher just as his son is deluded into thinking he could be an effective Member of Parliament.

If Dr. Pringle's judgment is blurred, in his own case, by vanity, it can also be adversely affected by narrowing influences exerted by the provincial culture which has helped to form the Minister's outlook, for that culture has its weaknesses as well as its strengths. In common with many of his parishioners, for example, Dr. Pringle tends to identify Christianity too uncompromisingly with Scottish Presbyterianism, its doctrines and prejudices. While not as extreme as the obvious bigots in his parish the Doctor, like his wife's correspondent Mally Glencairn, has "an orthodox corn or bunion" (II, 206) liable to become inflamed by particular secular and religious issues thus causing his attitudes toward these issues to be less open and tolerant than his views on moral and practical matters generally are.

To take a significant secular issue first, the puritanical view held by orthodox Presbyterians of the arts in general, and of the theatre in particular, predisposes the Minister against them. He feels obliged to justify his attendance at "the theatre of Drury Lane" in terms that he would not apply to the moral backsliders of his parish. He tells Mr. Micklewham:

> You must not think that I was there to see a carnal stage play, whether tragical or comical, or that I would so far demean myself and my cloth as to be a witness to the chambering and wantonness of ne'er-do-weel playactors.

He goes on to say that he visited the theatre in order to attend an oratorio, "...a most edifying exercise of psalmody and prayer" (II, 161). He is anxious to make it known that where "carnal" stage plays are concerned he is still in agreement with that local opinion which, he reminds his session-clerk, rejoiced when "a playhouse in Glasgow had been converted into a tabernacle of religion" (II, 160).

It is clear when the "editor" describes the reception of this letter in Garnock that Dr. Pringle has cause to reassure his friends that he is free of theatrical contamination. Mr. Micklewham fears to read aloud the Minister's account of the oratorio because some of the parish elders, while eager enough to argue points of doctrine do not, where the theatre is concerned, make fine distinctions. "The Doctor had been at the playhouse," the Session-clerk informs Mr. Snodgrass, and "Mr. Craig would be neither to bind or to hold when he heard that" (II, 159-60). The less "orthodox," more culturally enlightened young pastor (who has to read that "carnal" novel, *Ivanhoe,* in secret) sees things differently, especially after he has read Dr. Pringle's letter. The "editor" tells us that in Mr. Snodgrass's view since the Doctor "had not gone to the playhouse for the motives which usually take bad people to such places, he thought there could be no possible harm in reading the letter to the elders" (II, 165-66).

The difference between Dr. Pringle and his wife and the really bigoted members of their community is evident when one compares the elder Pringles to Mrs. Glibbans. "That ardent matron," as the "editor" calls her (II, 212), wrapping accusation transparently in a rhetorical question, renders Mr. Snodgrass speechless by asking him:

> What think you of this dining on the Lord's day, this playing on the harp, the carnal Mozarting of that ungodly family with whom the corrupt human nature of our friends has been chambering? (II, 152).

Her language resembles that applied by Dr. Pringle to "ne'er-do-weel playactors" but her verbal assault upon the Pringles' affable London hosts, her attack upon their "carnal" entertainment, had he heard it, would have left Dr. Pringle as much at a loss for words as Mr. Snodgrass. The doctor feels he must defend his visit to the theatre but he did visit it and he enjoyed the oratorio, a form of entertainment of which he had no previous experience. One cannot imagine either Mrs. Glibbans or Mr. Craig, with their rigid puritanism, ever crossing the threshold of "the theatre of Drury Lane."

The Minister's prejudices concerning high culture are not as firmly rivetted as those of some of his parish but he is as partisan as his most doctrinaire parishioners could desire when he discusses the Church of England.[17] In one letter he describes a visit to St. Paul's Cathedral and refers ecumenically to Christ as "Him before whom pope and presbyter are equal" (II, 113).[18] This promise of impartiality of judgment in church affairs vanishes quickly when the Minister decides that presbyters are more equal than those he dismisses as "the prelacy," a term that encompasses the Church of England and the Church of Rome alike for, later, he describes the Archbishop of Canterbury as "cousin german to the Pope of Rome" (II, 227). His brief call at the Cathedral leads him to reflect that "the Church of England is not so well reformed and purged as ours is from the abominations of the leaven of idolatry" (II, 113). The emptiness of the place causes him to conclude that "prelatical usurpations are on the downfall" (II, 114). This is good news to his congregation though Mr. Snodgrass has difficulty in stifling his amusement. It is highly ironic that toward the end of his stay in London Dr. Pringle is obliged in another epistle to the Garnockians to explain that his daughter, Rachel, was married in an Anglican church, "in a pagan fashion," as he phrases it (II, 260). He reassures his friends of the validity of Rachel's marriage by writing that he conducted the wedding ceremony over again in a manner "according to all regular marriages in our national church" (II, 260).

Dr. Pringle's attitude to the Church of England is coloured as much by Scottish nationalism as by doctrinal differences and nationalism, like Presbyterian orthodoxy, can put judgment in blinkers. Dr. Pringle's nationalistic antipathy to the Church of England gets him into political trouble as ironic as the difficulties into which he was led by his ill-judged though initially well-meant association with "the Saints." In theory the Minister is a political quietist, explaining to Mr. Micklewham:

> You know that politics are far from my hand: they belong to the temporalities of the community, and the ministers of peace and good-will to man should neither make nor meddle with them (II, 194).

In an earlier letter, however, he had made an exception to this generalization — an exception stemming from his loyalty to the Scottish church, and it is one which overturns the rule.

In that earlier letter he had written to his Session-clerk, like a latter-day Jeremiah, to declare that:

> If ever the time should come, in my day, of a saint-slaying tyrant attempting to bind the burden of prelatical abominations on our backs, such a blast of the gospel trumpet would be heard in Garnock as it does not become me to say. . .(II, 165).

The "backs" in question are those of Scottish Presbyterians and when he is in London Dr. Pringle fears that the "burden of prelatical abominations" is about to be bound on them. He hears that the Archbishop of Canterbury has countenanced an order in council forbidding the Scottish clergy to pray for the hapless Queen Caroline whose trial before the House of Lords was the most notable event of a notable year.[19] Dr. Pringle associates the persecution of the Queen with the persecution of the Scottish church at the hands of the English, and he is so emotionally involved with the Queen's cause that he regards impartiality of judgment as irrelevant. He declares to his Session-clerk:

> I made it a point never to read the evidence, being resolved to stand by THE WORD from the first, which is clearly and plainly written in the Queen's favour, and it does not do in a case of conscience to stand on trifles (II, 258).[20]

Far from remaining quiescent, according to his theory, Dr. Pringle decides it is time to blow "the gospel trumpet" and "meddle" with politics. In the absence of an actual trumpet he takes to bawling his support of the Queen and his defiance of authority with a mob in the street "...in spite of my decorum" (II, 260). He writes to say that he hopes his parishioners will not disapprove of his conduct but adds, rebelliously, "...whether they are satisfied or not, my conscience is content with me" (II, 259). This is not the case with his wife who is upset by her husband's association, out of a common desire to resist repression, with radical extremists he normally abhors. Writing to Mally Glencairn of the popular movement in support of the Queen she underlines the irony of her husband's position by asking her correspondent: "For, if it's a radikol job, as I jealoos it is, what will the doctor then say, who is an orthodox man, as the world nose?" (II, 253).

Dr. Pringle, of course, is motivated by genuine sympathy for the distressed Queen but he is subjected to irony for permitting the past — the past of such persecutions of the Scots by the English for religion's sake which Galt later dramatized powerfully in *Ringan Gilhaize* — to tinge his view of the present. The past, however, does not get in the way of the Minister's appreciation of the economic and technological advances of his day. In his small comunity, as we have seen, he is acquainted first-hand with poverty and thus is less inclined than his children to dismiss as ungenteel those who, in their commercial and industrial enterprises, were adding to the Kingdom's prosperity as well as to their own. From the outset the manifestations of modern "improvement" strike the Minister with admiration and awe. On his journey to Edinburgh he writes excitedly to Mr. Mickewham that:

> At Greenock I saw nothing but shipping and building; at Glasgow, streets spreading as if they were one of the branches of cotton-spinning; and here |Edinburgh) the houses grown up as if they were sown in the seed-time with the corn by a drill machine (II, 81).

Such a passage indicates that the new technology of the agricultural and industrial holds no terrors for Dr. Pringle;[21] in London, accompanied by his wife, he seeks out as many technological wonders as he can find. On his return to Garnock the Minister proposes an "improvement" of his own. Lining the road to welcome him back stand "'a batch of wabster lads,' with green aprons and thin yellow faces" (II, 265) suffering in consequence of a fall in trade. The sight of these dispirited men prompts the Minister to draw upon his newly-acquired knowledge of modern institutions which can at least supplement private philanthropy and other traditional sources of parochial assistance to the poor. He suggests, the "editor" records:

> The setting up of a lending bank in the parish for the labouring classes, where, when they were out of work, 'bits loans for a house-rent, or a brat of claes, or sic like, might be granted, to be repaid when trade grew better, and thereby take away the objection that an honest pride had to receiving help from the Session' (II, 271).

The Minister's customary benevolence, it is evident, predominates upon his return to his community. It is a benevolence, however, educated by more thorough self-knowledge and the wider experience afforded him by his change of environment. He has been humbled as a result of his vanity, having to confess to his Session-clerk:

> I have been governed by a spirit of ostentation, and not that lowly-mindedness without which all almsgiving is but serving the altars of Belzebub (II, 192).

In spite of his inherited puritanism he has been made aware that music and religion are not at strife, and that the spirit may be cultivated even in a theatre. He has seen the various manifestations of an emerging industrial society and acts upon the spirit of "improvement" as soon as he returns to his parish, using new tools in his old war against poverty. He has not been made perfect but the widening of his horizons cannot but improve his judgment. No doubt his loyalty to his church is as fierce on his return as it proved to be in London, and he is allowed his very human material vanities, all paid for by the legacy: the more expensive clothes, the new coach, and "the estate of Moneypennies" which is bought for him as a "great bargain" (II, 279). But the prideful vanity which afflicted him in London has been eradicated, the "editor" is at pains to emphasize. The latter informs the reader that the elders of Dr. Pringle's church agree that "being none lifted up, [he] was worthy of his rich legacy" (II, 273). Lest estate-buying seem overly ostentatious the "editor" explains that:

> It was not, however, on account of the advantageous nature of the purchase that our friend valued this acquisition, but entirely because it was situated in his own parish, part of the lands marching with the glebe (II, 279).

The Minister, after all, is about to retire and leave his parish in the care of the very able, compassionate and enlightened Mr. Snodgrass. Dr. Pringle, like Parson Adams, is welcomed home "...as a father returned to his children, and a king to his people" (II, 277), and the "editor" obviously considers this welcome a proper measure of the true worth of the Minister of Garnock.

Mrs. Pringle, like her husband, benefits from the experience of her journey, returning to Garnock to tell her friends that "travelling has, surely, a fine effect in enlarging the understanding" (II, 270). On a superficial view of her correspondence this declaration might be regarded as comically ironic, especially as she goes on to say that "...both the doctor and me thought, as we came along, that everything had a smaller and poorer look than when we went away" (II, 270). This undiplomatic rider to her comment upon the educative effect of travel seems consistent with Mrs. Pringle's "whorsogroffie," her advice to Mally Glencairn in one of her letters to be "more exac in your inditing, that no torbolashon may hippen on a future okashon" (II, 251), and her account of rebellious London servants of whom she writes: "...we were obliged to evacuate to their terms" (II, 196). Despite a certain amount of this kind of orthographical humour, however, Mrs. Pringle is not dismissed as a figure of fun. She is no Tabitha Bramble.[22] Not without justice, she lays claim to "forethought and wisdom" (II, 187). Her troubles with written language arise because speech is her usual mode of communication; unlike the letters of the rest of the family who have received a formal education hers, as Francis Hart observes, "...are struggles to set down speech."[23] Far from displaying ignorance in a comic fashion Mrs. Pringle illustrates the pragmatic common sense which Galt thought essential to sound judgment and which, upon occasion, signally fails to guide her husband or her children. Her wisdom is of the practical kind; as Mally Glencairn remarks: "Mrs. Pringle's a managing woman, and ye maunna expect any metaphysical philosophy from her" (II, 126).[24]

Mally is right. Mrs. Pringle's letters are full of the empirically observed detail that forms the texture of daily life. Writing to friends at home of the minutiae of London life Mrs. Pringle states: "I wantit to be partikylar, and to say nothing but what i saw with my own eyes" (II, 156). This attitude is much appreciated by those who hear her letters read aloud and who have been influenced by the same cultural forces. The recipients of her letters, the "editor" informs us, "unanimously agreed that Mrs. Pringle gave a more full account of London than either father, son, or daughter" (II, 130). Galt's approval of Mrs. Pringle's empiricism is evident in his refusal to submit it to the diminishing irony he reserves for the other members of the family when they wax "metaphysical."

Since Mrs. Pringle's interests are primarily domestic her letters contain accounts of household matters, comic in that she engages daily in a struggle with the practices, assumptions, and expectations of a culture foreign to her. Accustomed to thrift she finds it hard to cope with her new-found affluence in a society with a higher standard of living than that which she has temporarily left. She is justifiably anxious over the rash expenditures of her husband and son, not to mention the vagaries of the stock-market. She confides to Mally Glencairn that she wishes the money from the legacy were invested "in yird and stane, which is a constansie" (II, 252) and, as we have seen, ultimately she gets her way. If she is anxious about money, however, Mrs. Pringle has common sense enough not to become obsessed by it.

Mrs. Pringle is not rigidly confined to the house, as she makes plain when she writes to Mally Glencairn that:

> The doctor and me, by ourselves, since we have been settlt, go about at our convenience, and have seen far mae fairlies than baith Andrew and Rachel, with all the acquaintance they have forgathert with (II, 222).

The "fairlies" to which Mrs. Pringle refers are largely the technological wonders to be found in London. Her disappointment at her children's lack of interest in them is off-set by the satisfaction she gains by sharing her excitement at her discoveries with friends at home. She writes to them to describe the spectacle of gas lighting in the streets, and mentions a visit to a gas "manufactor"

— "...an awful place and, they say, as fey to a spark as poother" (II, 223). She records a visit to a brewery, and on another occasion she is impressed by "a curiosity of a steam-ingine that minches minchcollops as natural as life, and stuffs the sosogees itself" (II, 223). Every novelty is grist to Mrs. Pringle's mill. In a single paragraph she races breathlessly from Parliament to a printing press (preferring the latter) before hurrying on to describe household pets who wait for "wives going about with whirl-barrows, selling horses flesh to the cats and dogs by weight" (II, 224). The naive, unstructured manner in which Mrs. Pringle expresses her enthusiasm is amusing but her practical mind leads her, like her husband, to welcome technological change while those hidebound by tradition were resisting it.

When she first arrived in London, however, Mrs. Pringle was not quite so open-minded about her new environment. In an early letter to Nanny Eydent, Mantua-maker, of Irvine, she benevolently reports on the London fashions in clothes that the information "might be servisable to you in your bizness" (II, 156), but at the same time she admits "I am wearying to be back," advising Nanny that London "...is not a town for any creditable young woman like you to live in by yerself" (II, 158). To Mally Glencairn she complains that:

> It does not doo for a woman of my time of life to be taken out of her element, and, instead of looking after her family with a thrifty eye, to be sitting dressed all day seeing the money fleeing like scalte stones (II, 186).

Yet in spite of this complaint she now indicates a frustrated willingness to learn what she begins to perceive are valuable lessons that her new surroundings have to teach. She protests that:

> The Englishers are sae obstinate in their own way that I can get them to do nothing like Christians; and, what is most provoking of all, their ways are very good when you know them, but they have no instink to teach a body how to learn them (II, 184-5).

When, through observation and experience, she has learned more about English "ways" Mrs. Pringle writes in a quite altered tone that "I can see a better order and method really among the Londoners than among our Scotch folks, notwithstanding their advantages of edicashion" (II, 224).

Although she lacks the "advantages of edicashion" herself, Mrs. Pringle returns to Garnock with wider mental horizons, altered perspectives that diminish provincial narrowness in spite of her spelling. She would no more have endorsed a premature verdict passed by Mally Glencairn on her London adventure than her husband would have approved of Mrs. Glibbans's characterization of his London hosts and his metropolitan entertainment. After reading one of Mrs. Pringle's early letters to an assembled company Mally announces that:

> Riches do not always bring happiness; and poor Mrs. Pringle would have been far better

> looking after her cows and her butter, and keeping her lassies at their wark, than with all this galravitching and grandeur (II, 187).

The sentiment behind this declaration applies more properly to Rachel of whom even her friend Isabella is driven to remark that "... the acquisition of a fortune seemed to have brought out some unamiable traits in her character" which might have "slumbered, unfelt by herself and unknown to her friends" had she not been "exposed to the companions and temptations of the great world" (II, 183).

Where character and judgment are concerned Rachel is the antithesis of her parents. In her letters constantly, but inexpertly, she acts a part, laying claim to ideals in which she does not really believe but which she has garnered second-hand from the popular literature of her day. She is a parody of the heroine of sensibility who writes of "my too sensitive spirit" malice" than of sympathetic feeling.

Her supposedly "sensitive spirit" is attracted to the romantic medievalism which Scott made popular. On the way from Garnock to Greenock she sees some medieval ruins and in writing about them to Isabella throws herself into conventional ecstasy, exclaiming "What delightful ideas are associated with the sight of such venerable remains of antiquity!" She then proceeds to give an account of "the ancient castle of Skelmorlie" in what amounts to a brief, though on her part unintentional, parody of Scott. The castle, she writes, was the place:

> Where the Montgomeries of other days held their gorgeous banquets, and that brave knight who fell at Chevy-Chase came pricking forth on his milk-white steed, as Sir Walter Scott would have described him (II, 76).

Rachel soon makes it clear that her enthusiasm for what she terms "... those days of romantic adventure when to live was to enjoy a poetical element" (II, 76) arises less from sympathy with the ideals of chivalry than from her identification with the aristocracy "of other days." When, further along the road, she encounters the houses of the powerful West-county commercial aristocracy of her own days she ceases her dubious lament over a lost "age of chivalry" (II, 76) and turns instead to sneering. Forgetting that she and her family are en route to collect a fortune left them by a Nabob she writes contemptuously:

> We beheld, in all the apart and consequentiality of pride, the house of Kelly overlooking the social villas of Wemyss Bay. My brother compared it to a sugar hogshead and them to cotton-bags, — for the lofty thane of Kelly is but a West India planter, and the inhabitants of the villas on the shore are Glasgow manufacturers (II, 77).

Rachel is unaware that she is projecting her own pride upon the "new men" of her day whose accomplishments, as we have seen, are much admired by her parents.

Rachel's account of the funeral of George III demonstrates that her "sensibility" and "devotion" to chivalry are poses. She claims that the family attends the funeral "to pour the tribute of our tears upon the royal hearse" though, incongruously, she also writes that she promises herself "a day of unclouded felicity" (II, 148) owing to the anticipated presence of a certain Captain Sabre who has begun to pay court to her. When the Captain is unexpectedly called away to duty Rachel's day clouds over. Her attention is easily distracted from Windsor Castle, "so dear to chivalry," by her feeling that she has unjustly been robbed of enjoyment. She is left, she asserts in her letter," . . . pining with chagrin at the little respect paid by the rabble to the virtues of the departed monarch" (II, 148) though her "chagrin" is provoked more by the Captain's absence than the crowd's behaviour. Mrs. Pringle, with no private motive for pique, is more convincing in her indignation on that score; she bluntly describes those attending the funeral as ". . . an unreverent mob that scarsley could demean themselves with decency as the body was going by" (II, 157). Rachel's recriminations directed at the rest of her family as well as at the crowd indicate that selfishness rather than sensibility is at the root of her character.

Rachel rather fancies her intellect as well as that "too sensitive spirit" which enables her to find in medieval feudalism and its ruinous trappings a "poetical element" missing in a world of cotton manufacturers. She is thus given to uttering the current cant about "mind" as when, writing to Isabella, she asks with a rhetorical flourish: "and what are ladies and gentlemen without mind but a well-dressed mob! It is to mind alone that I am at all disposed to pay the homage of diffidence" (II, 181). When, elsewhere, she essays to describe "the intellectual portion" of the entertainment at a dinner party (II, 149) her own mind, however, wanders easily from the subject to focus upon Captain Sabre, a man not noted for his intellect. Rachel writes, ironically, that he is "not such a genius as my brother" (II, 151), and she has to admit to Isabella that he "has no literary partialities." In order to justify her interest in him, therefore, she is forced to resort to rationalization arguing conveniently, but with telltale defensiveness, that:

> Literary accomplishments are, you know, foreign to the military profession, and if the Captain has not distinguished himself by cutting up authors in the Reviews, he has acquired an honourable medal by overcoming the enemies of the civilized world at Waterloo (II, 151).

Rachel is found to prefer someone who cuts up Frenchmen rather than authors, thus clinging to "chivalry" while she abandons "mind." What she is basically attracted by, apart from his good looks, is the Captain's money, however. The devotee of "mind" writes that his "fortune is far beyond what I could ever have expected without the legacy, and equal to all I could hope for with it" (II, 179).

Rachel can see the faults in others with blinding clarity while her persistent vanity and pride ensure that she fails to recognize her own. In a letter commenting upon the metropolitan follies of her family she is critical of all but herself. "Andrew," she writes, "became a man of fashion, with all the haste that tailors, and horses, and dinners, could make him"; her father, she continues, "was equally inspired by lofty ideas and began a new career that promised a liberal benefaction of good things for the poor" and, she alleges, her mother "was almost distracted with calculations about laying out the money to advantage" (II, 236) though at the time of writing all three have recognized the errors of their conduct. Imperceptive of her own serious moral weaknesses, Rachel concludes her letter by declaring that "I alone preserved my natural equanimity" (II, 236) and remained "unseduced by the blandishments of rank" (II, 237). Rachel is self-deceived but she does not fool the recipients of the Pringles' letters. The contradictions between her words and deeds or her words and the real motives for her actions which she unconsciously reveals not only prompt Isabella's criticism, quoted earlier, but give rise to the view collectively held by the "chorus" and summarized by the "editor" that "there was a change in Rachel's ideas, and that it was not for the better" (II, 182-3).

It can be argued that from one point of view Rachel's "ideas" don't change enough for the good of her judgment. She fails to rid herself of the vanity and pride which are secularized forms of the spiritual arrogance that afflicts Mr. Craig and Mrs. Glibbans and her recorded opinions show that she does not transcend their parochial ignorance. Something of Mr. Craig's obsession with theatrical "carnality" is evident when Rachel stigmatizes the dancers at the opera as "...all foreigners who are, you know, naturally of a licentious character, especially the French women" (II, 179). Her unreasonable dislike of Mr. Argent's daughter resembles Mrs. Glibbans' daughter, Becky's, dislike of Rachel for in both cases it is based upon unacknowledged envy of another's good fortune. Rachel denigrates Miss Argent's musical skill, writing waspishly to Isabella that it "may be very well in a playactor or a governess that has to win her bread by music" (II, 181). It is curious, considering her odes to "mind," that Rachel can't understand how Miss Argent describes a countess as "ignorant and presuming" for, biased in favour of rank despite her assertion to the contrary, Rachel asks Isabella, "How is it possible that she can be so, as she is an earl's daughter, and bred up for distinction?" (II, 182).

Rachel eventually marries her Captain and departs on her honeymoon to Paris (capital city of the erstwhile "enemies of the civilised world" and haunt of "licentious" French dancers) with an enlarged fortune though not, like her parents on their return home, with an enlarged understanding. It depends upon character as to whether or not the stimulus of a new environment will broaden the apprehension of reality and improve the judgment.

In this respect Andrew Pringle is a more ambiguous figure than his sister. In some ways he learns to see life less parochially than on his arrival in London, but to the end he shares Rachel's social prejudices which, if anything, city life and new wealth reinforce. He is basically more perceptive than Rachel because although he is self-opinionated he is not as completely self-absorbed as she is. In defending him Mally Glencairn agrees that Andrew "deals in the diplomatics of obscurity" but she affirms that "in his own way, he kens the loan from the crown of the causey" (II, 140.[25]) He can be quite as foolish as his sister but the "editor" is willing to make allowances for Andrew that he does not make for Rachel. In a passage Galt added to the novel when it was re-published in book form the "editor" warns the reader:

> It would appear that the young advocate is not so solid in the head as some of his elder brethren at the Bar; and, therefore, many of his flights and observations must be taken with an allowance on the score of his youth (II, 84).

Andrew demonstrates almost at once, that, unlike his sister, he is capable of recognizing and admitting to mistaken judgment. As "legatees" the Pringles travel to the capital out of what Andrew terms "prudential considerations" (II, 98) – considerations that seem less prudent in London than in Garnock. Dr. and Mrs. Pringle make the journey to London to secure their inheritance for fear that Mr. Argent (the dead Nabob's agent) might be corrupt and try to defraud them of it. Andrew thinks this to be a very real possibility in spite of his recent legal training and supposed knowledge of "the world." Mr. Argent, however, is discovered to be honourable, affable, and business-like. Toward the end of their stay in London Mrs. Pringle writes of the Argents (ironically in view of her initial suspicions) that they are "a most discrit family, payin' to the last farding the cornal's legacy, and most seevil and well bred to us" (II, 251). Andrew, however, confesses at once that his and his parents' worries "were but the fantasms of our own inexperience." The family, he writes soon after reaching London, has been misled by what he calls "our provincialism" (II, 98).

Andrew, like Rachel, is given to rhaposdy upon the subject of chivalry but unlike his sister he separates fanciful musing from objective perception as his account of the king's funeral illustrates. Windsor Castle arouses Andrew's "enthusiasm" as well as Rachel's, suggesting to him "trains of thought and currents of feeling" which produce the effect of "sublimity" (II, 138) though both to his Garnock audience and to the reader his description of the scene at the castle is less sublime than ridiculous in its hyperbole. He writes:

> The towers, like the vast spectres of departed ages, raised their embattled heads to the skies, monumental witnesses of the strength and antiquity of a great monarchy. A prodigious multitude filled the courts of the venerable edifice, surrounding on all sides a dark, embossed structure, the sarcophagus, as it seemed to me at the moment, of the heroism of chivalry (II, 137).

If this passage is reminiscent of Rachel on the "ancient castle of Skelmorlie" Andrew soon admits that he has been indulging a subjective fancy for, he observes, ". . . in the visible objects of the funeral of George the Third there was but little magificence" (II, 138-9).

Andrew is most like his sister in his snobbery which distorts his judgment as it distorts hers. No less than Rachel he wants everyone to know that he keeps exalted company though his companions are "gentlemen" rather than aristocrats. There is a rather ironic tentativeness in his boastful report to Snodgrass that his companions are young men who "are looked up to as men of taste and refinement, and are received with a degree of deference that bears some resemblance to the respect paid to the hereditary endowment of rank" (II, 169-70).

Preoccupied with rank and genility Andrew, like Rachel, is contemptuous of men who dirty their ungentlemanly hands in "trade." He meets someone in whose face he discerns "traces of craft and dissimulation" because, as a stockbroker, the man is engaged in the "trade of moneymaking" (II, 124) — the "trade" which has helped to produce the money he spends so freely. Similarly, he notes a "wily cast" in the "pale countenance" of Wood, radical politician, Lord Mayor of London, and champion of the persecuted Queen Caroline.[26] Andrew concedes that Wood is a man of ability (Andrew, too, supports the Queen) but then dismisses him as one who "has neither the language nor the deportment of a gentleman." The Lord Mayor's ability lies in his "intuitive skill" which Andrew proceeds to define negatively as:

> a kind of instinct by which he is enabled to attain his ends, in defiance of a capacity naturally narrow, a judgment that topples with vanity, and an address at once mean and repulsive (II, 205).

In this strange assessment Andrew projects upon Wood some of his own weaknesses just as his sister projected hers upon the unsuspecting thane of Kelly and his manufacturing neighbours.

Andrew's observations are as unreliable when warped by political bias as they are when distorted by class prejudice. He tells Mr. Snodgrass that the young men with whom he associates "have a relish for intellectual pleasures, free from the acerbities of politics" (ii, 170) but this does not prevent him from being acerbic when he turns to political commentary. As Galt points out in his *Autobiography*, Andrew is an ultra-Tory who "under a show of candour. . . has strong prejudices."[27] For example, after quickly sketching some good qualities in Burdett and Hobhouse, candidates in the Westminister election, he soon becomes as critical of them as of Wood for all three offend Andrew's toryism by manifesting what he deems to be an undesirable "subjection to public opinion" (II, 202). Andrew pronounces that Hobhouse is "a political adventurer" whose cause is "Hobhouse *versus* Existing Circumstances" (II, 204) while Burdett is said to possess "the art of saying bitter things in a sweet way" though evidently a "way" not very intelligible for, Andrew proclaims, he "cannot utter a sequence of three sentences without violating common grammar" (II, 203).

Andrew is as orthodox politically as his father is ecclesiastically and finds himself in a parallel ironic dilemma. Radicalism is anathema to both yet Andrew, like his father, finds himself on the same side as the radicals in his support of the queen whose cause (perhaps fittingly) brings together strange bedfellows. Writing to Snodgrass of the Queen's plight he says that he has seen "with the admiration of a worshipper, the manner in which the multitude have espoused her cause" (II, 247). He praises the English people's "boundless generosity, which can only be compared to the impartial benevolence of the sunshine" (II, 246). It seems that Andrew is not immune to "public opinion" and since, in the queen's case, this "opinion" is radical in nature Andrew, like his sister, is forced to rationalization and, as with Rachel, brings patriotism to his aid. Of the Queen's supporters he writes that "there may be many among them actuated by what is called the Radical spirit" but, he argues:

> Malignity alone would dare to ascribe the bravery of their compassion to a less noble feeling than that which has placed the kingdom so proudly in the van of all modern nations (II, 246-7).

Andrew's compassion for the Queen does not moderate his political dogmatism, however, or make him generally more charitable or less snobbish.

Andrew's observations are at their most objective and reliable — less qualified by irony and least like Rachel's — when he "anatomizes" life in London from a provincial perspective. When he discusses metropolitan manners and morals critically but appreciatively; when he describes such phenomena as urban anonymity, egocentricity, and the rapid pace of city life; when he remarks upon the sheer incomprehensibility of the metropolitan scale, then he uses his judgment to advantage and shows, as Mally Glencairn asserted, that he "kens the loan from the crown of the causey" (II, 140). Where Rachel imposes her ready-made, insular notions upon what she sees in London Andrew is more even-handed, weighing the relative merits of the outstanding features of urban and rural life.

IV

The Ayrshire Legatees was originally intended to be a series of light topical sketches designed to entertain the reader by presenting a group of Scottish provincials come to London to see the "lions."[28] In the course of writing the work, however, Galt created a more serious though no less amusing novel than he had planned. Although writing of the immediate present, by focusing attention upon human character and upon the various socio-historical forces which help to shape character and to influence judgment, and by doing so with imagination, flair, and delicate artistry he turned a work that for the modern reader would otherwise hold only historical interest into a novel of lasting value. This was no inconsiderable achievement.

In *The Ayrshire Legatees* Galt, like Coleridge though more indirectly, suggests the need in a time of historical change for a balance between the principles of permanence and of progression for the sake of social order and well-being. The novel intimates that in the lives of individuals and in the larger life of society there must be a leavening of self-interest by benevolence; the individualistic drives of the capitalist must not be thwarted but, equally, they most not be permitted to eradicate or to replace the values associated with community and the rural past. Since Galt is a realist none of the characters in *The Ayrshire Legatees* manifests a perfect union of community feeling and either individual enterprise or an acceptance of its necessity, though the elder Pringles come closest to this ideal. They return to their village, however, leaving their more self-centred children in the city and this makes the novel's conclusion somewhat ambiguous. Perhaps the necessary rapprochement between the forces which make the stability and those which make for change is only possible in small communities?

Whatever Galt's original intentions may have been *The Ayrshire Legatees,* in its analysis of character and of the social environment, is a suitable prologue to the series of novels which its considerable success encouraged Galt to write, and which he called his "theoretical histories of society."[29] But prologue though it may be, and transitional work in the literary career of John Galt though it undoubtedly was, it is, more importantly, a well-formed novel the apparent simplicity of which masks its subtlety and penetration; it can stand on its own shapely feet. Critics of fiction — not of Scottish fiction only — should take another look at it.

NOTES

[1]Godfrey Frank Singer, *The Epistolary Novel: Its Origin, Development, Decline, and Residuary Influence* (New York, 1963), p. 216, p. 156. This edition is a re-issue of the original.

[2]See, for example, John Barth's novel *Letters* (New York, 1979).

[3]William Mills Todd III, *The Familiar Letter as a Literary Genre in the Age of Pushkin* (Princeton, 1976), p. 12.

[4]This is the view advanced by B.C. Southam in his book *Jane Austen's Literary Manuscripts* (Oxford, 1964). The quotation is taken from p. 58.

[5]As Singer points out, Galt was not the first to create such a hybrid but he was the first to manage it "with considerable aplomb." *Epistolary Novel,* p. 163.

[6]Galt uses this phrase in a letter to his publisher, Blackwood, dated 12 April, 1826. He writes: "If there is any merit in any of my sketches it is in the truth of the metaphysical anatomy of the characters." National Library of Scotland, MS 4017, f. 21. It should be noted that in an age when psychology was studied and taught as an element of moral philosophy Galt's "anatomy" naturally includes an analysis of values.

[7]"Bandana on Representation," *Blackwood's Edinburgh Magazine,* XV, No. Lxxiv (January, 1824), pp. 45-6.

[8]In his book on the Scottish novel Francis Russell Hart argues convincingly that Galt's theme is "the inescapable provinciality of human nature." See *The Scottish Novel, From Smollett to Spark* (Camb., Mass., 1978), p. 44.

[9]*The Literary Life and Miscellanies of John Galt,* 3 vols. (Edinburgh and London, 1834), I, 251. Even in *The Entail,* in which the narrator is supposedly omniscient, Galt

represents him as personally acquainted with the Walkinshaws and as telling a story of people he actually knew.

[10]After *The Ayrshire Legatees* Galt tended to use the memoir as a formal model though his novella, *A Rich Man* (1836), indicates that even toward the end of his life he could still handle the epistolary form interestingly.

[11]Quoted in William Mills Todd, *Familiar Letter,* p. 27.

[12]Galt's epistemology was strongly influenced by the thinking of the eighteenth-century School of Scottish Realism (or, as it is sometimes known, the Common Sense School). I have examined this influence at length in "The Community of Man: Galt and Eighteenth-Century Scottish Realism," *Scottish Literary Journal,* Vol. 8, No. 1 (May, 1981), pp. 10-29.

[13]Quoted in Robert Adams Day, *Told In Letters: Epistolary Fiction Before Richardson* (Ann Arbor, 1966), p. 201. Scott wrote this passage in his preface to Richardson's *Works* but he probably had in mind his novel *Redgauntlet,* his own experiment with epistolary fiction, published in the same year as the preface to Richardson (1824). Like *The Ayrshire Legatees* Scott's novel is a hybrid work, though one closer to "straight" narrative than Galt's.

[14]*The Works of John Galt,* D.S. Meldrum and William Roughead, eds., 10 Vols. (Edinburgh, 1936), II, p. 106. All other references to the novel are given in the text of the essay by volume and page number.

[15]The significance of the pastoral element in Galt's fiction has been discussed in my article "Early Remembrances: Pastoral in in the Fictional World of John Galt," *University of Toronto Quarterly,* XLVII, No. 4 (Summer, 1978), pp. 283-303.

[16]Richard Altick describes them as "a coterie of wealthy Church of England businessmen and their families known familiarly as the Clapham Sect (from the London suburb where they lived) and irreverently as 'the Saints'." *Victorian People and Ideas* (New York, 1973), p. 180.

[17]It is one of the many silent ironies of the novel that in spite of his vigorous denunciations of Anglicanism Dr. Pringle, by his association with "the Saints," preaches in an Anglican church and makes common cause for a time with a group within the Church of England, albeit an evangelical group.

[18]Dr. Pringle's visit to St. Paul's Cathedral is not simply that of a tourist; it is a reminder of a mock-heroic relationship which Galt quietly establishes between the Minister and the apostle. At the beginning of the novel, after hearing Dr. Pringle's account of his stormy voyage to London read aloud, a parishioner remarks, the editor tells us, that "he had not heard of greater tribulation by the waters since the ship-wreck of the Apostle Paul" (II, 94). Dr. Pringle's "espistles" contain admonitions not unlike those which St. Paul addressed to such recipients as the Corinthians while the Minister's confession, quoted later in the text of the essay, acknowledging that he has been governed by "a spirit of ostentation," is a brief paraphrase of St. Paul's celebrated definition of Christian charity. The generally submerged analogies between Dr. Pringle and St. Paul are not made to deprive the Minister of moral stature but to indicate that he is not a saint, though he is a good man; that his sphere of influence is local and restricted like that of most people. Occasionally, the analogies prick the Minister's pretentions. In *Annals of the Parish* similar analogies between the Rev. Mr. Balwhidder and George III serve similar purposes.

[19]In a year which saw the Cato Street Conspiracy, a call to revolution in Glasgow, the trial of Orator Hunt and other radicals for their part in the Peterloo massacre of the previous year, the inquiry into the Queen's conduct instituted by George IV with a view to dissolving his marriage and preventing his wife from being crowned became a *cause celebre* for radical opinion. The people saw the Queen as a fellow-sufferer under a repressive regime. Galt's focus upon the change of monarchy rather than upon the

yet more sensational events of 1820 indicates his desire to represent, as far as historical events would allow, the ordinary in everyday life rather than the sensational but ephemeral.

[20]It is interesting to note that Wilberforce, whom Dr. Pringle innocently terms "the chief Saint" (II, 163), was just as prepossessed in the Queen's favour. But this was in spite of his reading of the evidence, which obliged him to remark: "I fear she has been very profligate." Quoted in Sir Llewellyn Woodward, *The Age of Reform 1815-1870,* Second Edition (Oxford, 1962), p. 68.

[21]In Galt's fictional world the new technology is opposed with superstitious fervour by the reactionary Lairds whose position was threatened by it. This is evident in most of Galt's Scottish novels, but especially in *Sir Andrew Wylie* and in *The Last of the Lairds.*

[22]*The Ayrshire Legatees* is often compared to *Humphry Clinker,* another novel in which two generations of one family go on their travels and write to friends about what they see. The likeness of the two novels is, however, only superficial. *Humphry CLinker,* though epistolary in form, could easily be altered to become a third person narrative whereas *The Ayrshire Legatees* is too thoroughly epistolary for any such alteration. Further, beneath a superficial resemblance, the main characters are very different. In Galt's novel the reception of the Pringles' letters is a important as the letters themselves but in Smollett's work the reader is presented with the letters alone. They are letters for the most part written by characters who act as masks for the novelist; they write as if they were writing segments of a novel the plan of which is known in advance of the writing.

[23]*The Scottish Novel,* p. 34.

[24]Galt uses the word "metaphysical" in two different ways, though in both cases in relation to theory. He was contemptuous of "metaphysical philosophy" (Kant's, for example) as were the Scottish Realists for Galt and the Realists regarded metaphysical speculation as dubious because they thought it owed more to the imagination, and to fantasy, then to the observation of particulars on which their theories of knowledge were founded. When Galt uses the word "metaphsyical" in a positive sense (as in the phrase used in the title of this essay) he refers to theory based upon observation and the subsequent analysis of what has been observed.

[25]Literally, he can distinguish the middle of the road from the side (see Galt's *The Provost,* chaps. XV and XXVII). Metaphorically, Andrew is perceptive; he "knows what's what."

[26]Alderman Wood — to George IV "that beast Wood" — travelled to France to advise Queen Caroline to come to London. She came under his escort, entering the city on 6 June, 1820. See Woodward, *The Age of Reform,* pp. 67-68.

[27]*The Autobiography of John Galt,* 2 vols. (London, 1833), II, p. 229.

[28]See Galt, *Literary Life,* I, p. 227. In the introduction to his story "The Dean of Guild" (1833) Galt refers to *The Ayrshire Legatees* as "as kind of light writing, like caricature in drawing, with just so much of true portraiture as may render the outlines amusing, while the extravagance remains so obvious that to the soberest reader the fiction is not equivocal." *John Galt: Selected Short Stories,* Ian Gordon ed. (Edinburgh, 1978), p. 49. This may be an account of his initial intention but it is not an accurate description of his finished work. Galt was never a good judge of his own work, as he often admitted, and here he tries to dissociate himself from Andrew's political commentary which was "equivocal" enough to make many believe that in some cases he spoke directly for his creator.

[29]*Autobiography,* II, p. 219.

The narrative perspective of *The Last of the Lairds*

H.B. de Groot

Critics have always recognized Galt's ability in making his protagonists relate the story of their own lives. "As a fictitious autobiographer," a reviewer wrote as early as 1831, "Mr. Galt surpasses every writer, certainly of this day, perhaps of any time."[1] A few years earlier still William Blackwood, Galt's own publisher, had at the time that Galt was working on *The Entail* tried to discourage him from writing his novel in any other way:

> I hope you will be able to manage it so as that the hero tells the story himself for your may depend upon it, that it is always the most effective way, and is particularly your forte. You more than any one almost I know, identify the individual, and the Author himself never appears, it is the very being telling his story himself. This is greatly lost when given in the third person.[2]

In that comment Blackwood sensitively registers some of the distinctive qualities of Galt's narrative method but as a general piece of advice his statement was less than helpful. In suggesting that Galt should avoid experimentation and should stick to what he did well, Blackwood was restricting his novelist unduly. Moreover, he was hardly consistent. It was he who had insisted when Galt was working on *Sir Andrew Wylie* that Galt move away from the documentary chronicle format and concentrate on working out a "good and striking story"[3] – pressure which he reluctantly and unwisely gave way to. He did not make that mistake again with *The Entail* which he worked out in a very different manner. When he came to write *The Last of the Lairds* he went back to a first-person narrative but not that of the fictional autobiography, that is to say, not one in which the central character tells his own story.

It would seem that originally he *had* intended to write his novel that way. In the final chapter of *Sir Andrew Wylie* it is revealed that the old Laird of Craiglands, "the last of an ancient line," has on his death left a manuscript which in the words of his sister contains "a most full account of all manner of particularities anent the decay of the ancient families of the west country."[4] It would seem from this that what became *The Last of the Lairds* had originally been thought of as a kind of chronicle in which the Laird looked back on his life and times, the third in a series of fictional autobiographies – a series of which *Annals of the Parish,* published a year earlier, formed the first part and *The Provost,* still incomplete but already announced for publication, the second.

In the end much work, literary and otherwise, intervened and Galt did not return to the story of the last of the lairds for another three years. D.M. Moir, Galt's friend and Blackwood's literary adviser, wrote towards the end of the summer of 1825 to Blackwood that he and Galt had had "some conversation whether it would be better to make a novel of it, or a personal narrative."[5] This comment suggests that for Moir the novel and the fictional autobiography were distinct and mutually exclusive categories and that he associated the novel with third-person narrative and perhaps too with a more complex plot, so that for him *Sir Andrew Wylie* and *The Entail* would be novels as opposed to the *Annals* and *The Provost.*

Moir, on seeing the manuscript, had apparently thought that the Laird and his man Jock were the best things in it and had wished there to be more of them. But Galt, in a letter of 1 October 1826, disagreed:

> Beings like Jock and the Laird will not stand bringing out. There is something in imbecility that will not suffer it to endure much handling. The Laird's character has cost me more pains and reflection than any thing I ever attempted. I began the work as an autobiography, and, after having made considerable progress, threw it into the fire. The station of the Laird in society affords but few incidents, and the selfish stupidity of the person is too offensive in itself to interest. To avoid disgusting, is as much as one can hope for in delineating such a being.[6]

Moir would continue to see the change in narrative method as a mistake and he wrote a few years after Galt's death:

> Unfortunately the author was, somehow or other, induced to make the book a narrative instead of an autobiography, and thus deprived it, notwithstanding its general merits, of much of that *vraisemblance,* that apparent truth to nature, which lend such a charm and warmth to the characters just mentioned [Mr. Balwhidder in the *Annals*, Mr. Pawkie in *The Provost* and Mr. Duffle in *The Steamboat*].[7]

"Somehow or other" are rather extraordinary words to use since Moir himself quoted the letter in which Galt had spelled out his reasons for making the change. Moir's opinion is very close to Blackwood's here: there is one thing that Galt did supremely well and he ought to have stuck to it. The narrative method, however, which Galt finally decided on for *The Last of the Lairds* was one in which the 'I' is both an observer and a minor character in the story.

When Galt wrote that he had thrown an earlier 'autobiographical' version of the novel into the fire, he may well have been speaking metaphorically, for there is one section of the novel, the seventh chapter, in which the narrator presents us with a surreptitiously made copy of the Laird's own narrative, covering part of his early life. It is the one part of the novel in which the narrative method is rather clumsily handled and it may well represent a portion of an earlier version of the book which Galt, not a man likely to throw things away, was determined to salvage.[8]

In considering how Galt's conception of the Laird and of the best way of presenting his story evolved, it is necessary to go back once more to *Sir Andrew Wylie.* No one has ever found much good to say about its middle sections, the high-life intrigues and the melodramatic complications which Galt, probably at the instigation of Blackwood, grafted on to his originally much simpler structure. I would argue, however, that the problems in the novel go deeper and are in part related to the question of point-of-view. Galt rejected the first-person form, the 'fictional autobiography,' but never resolved whether to present Wylie's experiences through an omniscient narrator, whether explicitly brought forward or implied, or through a more limited first-person view. Most of the novel implies an omniscient authorial perspective but on occasion Galt introduces a point-of-view which is more limited and more precisely defined. Thus in the tenth chapter Andrew, in the course of his journey to London, visits and stays with the Glasgow "fabricator of muslins" Mr. Treddles, an event which allows the narrator to present Treddles' later memory of Andrew as a boy by repeating what Treddles told him "at the last Circuit." The narrator re-enters the novel on a few later occasions, notably towards the end where he reveals that as a child he grew up in the area and was involved in the mutilation of the old family mausoleum of the Lairds of Craiglands, and again in the final chapter where he is actually present when the clergyman, formerly the dominie, Mr. Tannyhill, is examining the children on their scriptural knowledge.[9] These narrative devices, however, are not used with sufficient consistency either to authenticate the scenes or to create a sense of the narrator's identity.

A second and a larger problem with *Sir Andrew Wylie* has to do with Galt's attitude towards the progatonist and towards his experience. In the best of Galt's first-person narratives we have a continuous interplay between the way in which the narrator presents himself and the effect which that presentation achieves. We see this interplay at its most subtle in *The Provost* when Pawkie convinces himself and tries to convince the reader that the interest of the self and the interest of the community coincide.

Sir Andrew Wylie lacks this kind of irony. The hero is a young Scot of a very humble background who goes to London, determined to make his way up which is exactly what he does. In London his total lack of sophistication strikes people as amusing. He is shrewd enough, however, not to allow people to treat him simply as a butt but instead he is able to use his energies, his directness, his apparent simplicity and his capacity to ingratiate himself as a way of getting on in the world.[10] It is as if the theme of *Great Expectations* is given if the theme of *Great Expectations* is given to us without any irony: Andrew is not, of course, given great expectations but he is certainly able to seize upon possibilities. In Dickens' novel Pip finds that his expectations dissolve like his own marsh mists and finds, just as painfully, that the way back to the by now idealized childhood no longer exists. He resolves to marry the girl whom he now feels he should have married, returns to what is no longer his home, and finds her a wife already. Andrew, on the other hand, gains money, aristocratic status and a political position. Having done so, he can afford to give up business and politics, to go back to Scotland and to marry the Laird's daughter, his own childhood playmate.

At the beginning of the novel Andrew was contemptuous of the old Laird: "he was . . . 'a carle that daunered about the doors wi' his hands in his pouches, and took them out at meal-time' " (I, 14). There is no indication that Galt feels at all differently about the old Laird and all he stands for. When Andrew goes back, he finds the Laird prejudiced — in a stupid and ignorant rather than in a malicious manner — against people whose money and position have not been inherited. Andrew is at first indignant but then mellows: "He was perfectly persuaded that the Laird, with all his faults and foibles, was in the main possessed of many of the homely virtues that befit the character of a resident landlord" (III, 282).

Shortly before this the Laird has had an accident in which his carriage overturns and in which he does not appear to be very hurt. But he is — he is unwillingly led to his bed and he does not recover. At his funeral the whole community comes to pay tribute to him, not so much to him personally as to him as the last representative of an acient family. There is also present at the funeral an old family retainer, as much the last of his line as the Laird whom he served. Thus the sense of the passing of an era is underlined. But the kind of social change set up is really of a very limited kind. Sir Andrew Wylie of That Ilk has now joined the landed gentry of South-West Scotland. Now that he has achieved money and status he can afford to be sentimental about the old gentry. In this Galt can simultaneously celebrate the energy of the self-made man and pay tribute to the old feudal world. The two impulses are not resolved, nor is the tension between them explored in any interesting way.

Malachi Mailings, the Laird of Auldbiggings, the central character of *The Last of the Lairds,* is also presented as the last descendant of a once powerful family. His estate is mortgaged to the hilt and its upkeep is terribly neglected. Since Galt thought that the Laird's awareness would be too limited for the novel to be told through his point-of-view, he invented a secondary character as the novel's narrator: a bachelor author, possibly a novelist, who lives in or near Paisley and who possesses a curiosity about people which is perhaps natural to a writer. Indeed one constantly feels that he looks at people as copy. Often, in a rather knowing and superior way, he invites the reader to be amused with him by the other characters. Thus, in the fifth chapter, he encourages Jock, the Laird's man, to consider himself the Laird's literary adviser, adding to the reader: "I had in this my mind's eye on Molière's Old Woman," a reference apparently to the well-known anecdote about Molière, who was said to put greater trust in his old servant's response to his writing than in that of more erudite listeners.[11]

At other times he presents himself as very much *au fait* with the latest literary, artistic and political gossip. He knows, for instance, the price Robert Peel paid for a Rubens painting. He does not tell us what it is — Professor Gordon does so in a helpful footnote (67) — but he writes about it in a knowing way which suggests that he could easily do so if he wished. At other time he writes in a self-consciously literary and rather old-fashioned way — a way which allows him to show off his wit, his sense of style, his political cynicism. The following passage, for instance, serves as much to characterize the narrator as it does to describe the Laird's house:

> At the far end was the court-house, in which, when the day happened to be wet, the poultry were accustomed to murmur their sullen and envious whiggery against the same weather which made their friends the ducks as garrulous with enjoyments at the midden-hole, as Tories in the pools of corruption.(2)

Here is a comparison between the old and the new clergyman of the parish, given through the difference between their gardens:

> Mr. Firlot's taste belonged indeed to another age and generation — he was one of those theological worthies who divided their sermons into fifteen heads, and planted in the same flower-beds cauliflowers and carnations. The pulpit became paralytic under his emphatic logomachies; and docks and nettles grew as rankly in all his borders, as epithets unpleasant to ears polite flourished in the mazes of his doxology. The docks and nettles, under the auspices of his more refined successor, had now given place to roses and lilies. The pulpit was repaired, and the desk thereof beautified with a new covering; the weedy pathway to the Manse door was trimmed into a gravelled sweep edged with box, and alternate tassels of red and white daisies, interspersed with flowers of rarer name and richer blossom, adorned the bed within. (42-43)

The analogy between the flowerbeds and the sermons is ingeniously sustained but the ingenuity is always kept in check by a sense of what is appropriate in the best Augustan manner. Indeed the poetic inversion "ears polite," possibly of semi-proverbial status in the early 1800s, derives ultimately from Pope's fourth *Moral Essay:* "To rest, the Cushion and soft Dean invite,/Who never mentions Hell to ears polite."[12]

Scott had set a pattern for the use of Scots and English by using Scots for dialogue and English for narrative. This inevitably created a series of rather abrupt transitions. Galt, in the *Annals* and *The Provost,* had been able to avoid the abruptness by having a provincial Scot tell his own story. By choosing narrators with some education and social status, he was able to avoid extreme problems of intelligibility which would have occurred if his narrators had spoken broad dialect. Even so, the more thorough use of Scots had tended to reduce the accessibility of the novels South of the border, a disadvantage which can be seen as the cost which the greater stylistic consistency of his novels had brought with it. In some of Galt's other novels he can descend to a very artificial kind of English — it happens, for instance, in the English aristocratic scenes in *Sir Andrew Wylie,* where it affects the dialogue as well as the narrative. In *The Last of the Lairds* language is used more subtly to place characters: the servants (Jock, Jenny Clatterpans, Leezy) speak a fairly broad Scots as do the older characters of higher social standing (the Laird himself; Mrs. Soorocks, who is the "relict" of a laird and herself the daughter of a heritor; the sisters Minnigaff who live on their own small estate). On the other hand, we find English spoken by the Nabob, who was born in the area but has lived most of his adult life in Indian; by Dr. Lounlands, the clergyman, even though he too is a local man of very humble parentage[13]; by Mr. Tawsie, the schoolmaster; by Mr. Loopy, the Glasgow lawyer; and by Mr. Coball, the stranger, who may be an Englishman, even if he can recognize an Aberdonian accent when he hears one.

In this world the deliberate use of English idioms and English pronunciations can be part of a put-down, an attempt to attain superiority, as in the following conversation between Mrs. Soorocks and Girzie Minnigaff:

> "Weel, leddies," said Mrs. Soorocks, "since it must be sae, what can we do but submit, — I think, Miss Shoosie, ye give baith the sore stroke and the loud cry; howsever, since it is a' past, and we're friens again —" "Friends!" cried Miss Girzie, with an English accent — "Friends! we may forgive what's past but I see no obligation for us to be friends." (128)

Very soon after, Miss Girzie returns to her normal speech: "it's what I never could alloo — twa clandestine marriages in my father's family" (129).

The narrator speaks English but he must be a Scot. He uses the word "jealousy" in the Scottish sense of suspicion (33), describes the laird as "like an Edinburgh advocate" warsling with the law" (6), and, at the end of the book, writes that the laird and his wife live in Edinburgh during "the season" but return home "to hain" for the winter (163). Occasionally he makes a point of introducing Scottish forms when addressing dialect speakers as in this dialogue with Leezy, Mrs. Soorocks' servant:

> "Weel, Leezy," said I, "which o' your sweethearts has led ye sae far a-field the night?" "Sweethearts! — the last sweetheart I had was a gingerbread fairing and I ate it." "O had I been made o' gingerbread, and in such lips!" replied I, in the tone of Romeo, wishing himself a glove. "Ye would hae been o' some use," retorted Leezy; "but I have na time the night to haver wi' you..." (89-90)

In his mixture of condescension and flirtatiousness he is rather heavy-handed and Leezie easily gets the better of him. At other times carefully chosen Scottish words are presented as if in quotation marks, when the narrator refers to Mrs. Soorocks' "smeddum," (113) for instance, or describes the entrance of "the kitchen, *anglice* tea-urn" (109). The way in which the narrator can move from one linguistic level to another becomes a way of placing him, of showing how he is both part of his society and yet stands outside it, how he is involved with it but can also regard it with condescension.

One asks oneself whether one should think of the narrator as Galt himself and Galt encourages one to ask that question while equivocating about the correct answer through a constant interplay between documentary and fictional detail, very much in the manner of the *Blackwood's Magazine* group to which Galt himself belonged, even if he was never very close to its centre. In *The Ayrshire Legatees,* for instance, a work originally published in *Blackwood's Magazine,* Dr. Pringle on his stopover in Edinburgh has "dinner in Macgregor's hotel, a remarkable decent inn, next door to one Mr. Blackwood, a civil and discreet man in the bookselling line."[14] In *The Gathering of the West* Galt names three of the bailies of the town of Leith, Bailie Macfie, Bailie Reoch and Bailie Newton, and he is particularly interested in Bailie Macfie, pointing out "how truly worthy indeed the town of Leith was to receive his Majesty, and how fortunate in having a Greenock gentleman at the head of his Magistracy; for it is well known, at least to all Greenock folk, that there are no such clever people as themselves anywhere in the know world."[15] That is a Greenock man, at least by adoption (Galt's family moved to Greenock when he was ten), speaking — not without irony — about his fellow-townsmen.

In these instances Galt introduced into the fictional world of his novels elements from an existing world of small towns. At other times Galt introduced details which appear real but may not be so. In the *Blackwood's Magazine* versions of *The Ayrshire Legatees* and of its sequels, *The Steamboat* and *The Gathering of the West,* we find a series of responses by readers. Professor Gordon takes these as showing how convincing Galt's documentary realism was[16] but I strongly suspect that most if not all of these were made-up. It is hard to believe in the reality (outside fiction) of a correspondent who questioned the veracity of the author by pointing out that there was no Miss Mally Glencairn living in the Kirkgate in Irvine[17] or the correspondent from Liverpool who expressed the hope that future episodes of *The Steamboat* would not include anything umpleasant about his town.[18] In these cases what may at fist sight appear to strengthen the documentary realism of Galt's novels ultimately does the opposite: it underlines their fictionality.

When Galt adapted *The Ayrshire Legatees* for publication as a book, he would have preferred to retain the letters from correspondents and his answers to them. But Blackwood thought otherwise. When Moir saw *The Last of the Lairds* through the press he also eliminated many of the topical references, partly to get rid of some of what he (and Blackwood) considered vulgarity and to eliminate personal references of a quasi-slanderous nature but also in order to turn the book into a self-contained novel as opposed to a work which constantly crossed and re-crossed different levels of reality. Moir cut out, for instance, the comments of William Jerdine's *Literary Gazette* (113) and he altered Galt's sly attempt to father his own story *The Omen* on Lockhart (87), although the joke is very much in the tradition of *Blackwood's Magazine* writers such as Wilson, Maginn and Lockhart himself.

Moir also cut a long passage about the uproar at Renfrew in Chapter 23. Here Galt's original version, now restored to us by Professor Gordon, relates how a riot had occurred because some "hempies" from Paisley had said rude things about the Renfrew steeple. The narrator pricks up his ears at this point for, he says, he has always been interested in steeples even if some are better than others. He has never thought much of the one at Port Glasgow and he will never be popular in a particular part of Glasgow itself, for he once called the steeple at Hutchesons' Hospital "a potatoe beetle" (96-9).[19] There clearly was a strong sense of rivalry among the various towns of the Clyde Valley and in his apparently irrelevant discussion of steeples Galt is once more playing his part as a Greenock man. In *The Ayrshire Legatees* Rachel Pringle had referred to Port Glasgow as "an insignificant town, with a steeple"[20] and the gibe is converted into heavily ironical praise of the steeple, with a comparison with the tower of Pisa thrown in, in the "notes to correspondents" that appeared in *Blackwood's Magazine* for October 1820.[21] *The Steamboat* returns to the matter of the Port Glasgow steeple on two occasions[22] by which point it has become a running gag.

We have seen how in *Sir Andrew Wylie* Galt showed his divided attitude to the old laird and what he represented. In *The Last of the Lairds* he was able to objectify this divided attitude by showing the changes in his narrator's sympathies. At the beginning of the book he is thoroughly contemptuous of the old Laird and he is also horrified by what he thinks of as the man's moral insensitivity, his ability to bear grudges years and years after events that prompted them. Yet when the nabob tries to foreclose the mortgage which he holds on the Laird's land and even jumps the gun by beginning to survey the land as if he already owns it, the narrator is rather shocked by this violation of "public decorum" (33) and he gradually becomes involved in attempts to extricate the Laird from his predicament. Mrs. Soorocks, the local busybody, and the narrator decide that the only way out is to marry the Laird to the elder of the Misses Minnigaff, even though the Laird finds her particularly unappetising. But when Mrs. Soorocks threatens to reveal the trouble the Laird has in the past had with the kirk-session, he gives in:

> "I canna," said he, in soliloquy, "warsle wi' this — I hae lang thole't the consperacy that has rookit my rents — I hae endur't the loss o' my first love, Annie Daisie — I quietly submitted to my wife till it pleased Providence to quench her — I hae seen the lands o' my forefathers mouldering awa — I hae known the terrors o' the law, and the judgment o' a wadset — I hae had sickness o' heart, and the rheumatics, and the toothache — Weel may I say wi' the play-actor in the show that I alloot in our barn, —
>
> 'But it's this too solid flesh which makes the calamity of life,
> For who would bear the pangs of despised love —
> The oppressor's wrong — the insolence of Law.'
> The Deevil tak Hugh Caption and all the other ills that flesh is heir to — I'm ruin't beyond redemption — Mrs. Soorocks and Sir — I gie myself up into your hands — be pityful if ye can." (112)

A distinct pathos mingles with the preposterous juxtapositions and the garbled Shakespearean quotations. Further complications arise and when the Laird's financial ruin seems imminent the narrator finds him in the middle of a melodramatic farewell to his garden:

As he walked along the dank unmoved grass, he paused suddenly, and stooping forward, he pulled a rose.
"It's my ain yet," said he with a smile, as he turned round and smelling it, held it out towards me.
"It has grown in my forefathers' land," he added, "I got the slip frae Castlesemple garden — I set it mysel — I made the hole for't wi' my ain very finger — I watered it wi' the china jug that was my father's punch porringer, as I hae heard my kind mother say — and what can be a man's ain, if that bush and bud be na mine?" (132-3)

The narrator himself comments:" the distress of his mind though visibly mingled with a strong ingredient of absurdity was yet such as could not be seen without sympathy" (132), rather frigid words for the elegiac quality that the novel has achieved, a shift in presentation not unlike that in Scott's account of the Baron of Bradwardine in *Waverley*. The elegiac quality is further accentuated when, in the next chapter, we have a detailed description of Mrs. Soorocks' cupboard, of "what in Renfrewshire was called a dining room press" (137), the use of the past tense is significant.[23]

The novel does not, however, end on this note. When it is discovered that money can be made out of selling the "superiority" or voting rights of the estate and when the Laird finds that his new wife is an extremely shrewd bargainer, he is now rather pleased with her and finds that he can now use the proceeds of his sale to go and live in style in the New Town in Edinburgh. The change in mood is deftly handled. If the effect of Scott's novels depends in part on his divided attitude towards energetic and adaptable survivors like Bailie Nicoll Jarvie on the one hand and doomed romantics like Redgauntlet on the other, Galt, who in *Sir Andrew Wylie* had seemed to be largely dismissive of the older world, has now found a way to revalue that world but also to show how someone like the old Laird can be both relic and survivor.

Galt's skill and originality as a documentary realist have always been recognized. Some readers — Coleridge among them — have noted the psychological insight with which Galt can portray the plausible self-delusions of his characters.[24] Ian Gordon, in his critical biography, has suggested two other ways in which Galt was an innovator: the way in which characters could be carried over from one book to another as in the *roman fleuve* later developed by Trollope and others; and the exposé of political life, locally in *The Provost,* nationally in *Sir Andrew Wylie* and — more consistently — in *The Member,* a way of writing in which Galt originated the genre of the political novel which one associates with Disraeli and Trollope. It has also been suggested that Galt's loosely constructed quasi-documentary long short-stories may have had an influence on a Canadian fictional tradition, perhaps directly on Haliburton and

McCulloch, indirectly on writers like Leacock and Alice Munro.[25]

I would like to add a further suggestion. I know of no precedent nor of any other example until the beginning of the twentieth century of a novel narrated by a minor character in which the narrator's changing attitudes to his subject are made central.[26] It is true that many eighteenth and early nineteenth century novels used the formula of a novel in which a fictional editor prepared for publication the papers of some fictitious narrator — it was, of course, Scott's favourite form and something rather like it had been done by Galt in the periodical version of *The Ayrshire Legatees* — but in such novels the narrator really belongs to the frame only. He appears at the beginning and may or may not reappear at the end but is lost sight of in between. Galt's method is much closer to that of Ford Madox Ford's *The Good Soldier* or to that of some of Conrad's novels, the last part of *Under Western Eyes,* for instance, or *Lord Jim* and other novels narrated by Marlow. It is no accident that these early modernists rebelled against the omniscient narrator or the first-person narrative, for in their novels the extent to which reality is knowable is itself their subject-matter. Conrad's Marlow makes this question in a very self-conscious way central to his way of narrating; Galt's annonymous narrator finds himself much to his own surprise on the side of a man for whom initially he had nothing but half-amused contempt. One could go on to say that Galt is less of an artist than Conrad, that like his narrator he himself blundered into something which he had hardly foreseen and could not be bothered to explore. (After all, as we have seen, as late as October 1826 Galt found only "imbecility" in the Laird.) But as in the case of the *roman fleuve* and that of the political novel it is Galt who pioneered a method in which it was left to later novelists to find a greater potential.[27] Galt was right to reject Moir's advice about the novel's narrative point-of-view but it is a pity that he was in no position to hold out against him when it came to seeing the novel through the press. But by then, of course, Galt was a long way away and was doing other important pioneering work in the backwoods of Upper Canada.

NOTES

[1]Anonymous critic in *The Spectator* 4 (14 May, 1831) 474, quoted by Bradford Booth in the Introduction to his edition of Galt's *The Gathering of the West* (Baltimore: Johns Hopkins Press, 1939), p. 35n.

[2]Quoted in Ian A. Gordon, *John Galt: The Life of a Writer* (Edinburgh: Oliver and Boyd; Toronto: University of Toronto Press, 1972), p. 55.

[3]Gordon, *John Galt: The Life of a Writer,* p. 42.

[4] John Galt , *Sir Andrew Wylie of That Ilk* (Edinburgh: William Blackwood; London: T. Cadell, 1822), III, 309. Subsequent references to *Sir Andrew Wylie* will be to this edition.

[5]Quoted by Ian A. Gordon in the Introduction to his edition of *The Last of the Lairds* (Edinburgh and London: Scottish Academic Press, 1976), p. viii. Subsequent references to *The Last of the Lairds* will be to this edition.

[6]"Biographical Memoir" prefixed to John Galt, *The Annals of the Parish and The Ayr-*

shire Legatees (Edinburgh and London: William Blackwood and Son, 1868), p. xl. The Memoir was first published in 1841.

[7]"Biographical Memoir," p. xxxix.

[8]In January 1826 Galt published, in the *Literary Souvenir* "A Feeling Neighbour: A Fragment," in which the busybody Mrs. Soorocks announces with glee to the Misses Minnygaff that they may shortly be dispossessed. The compositional relationship between the fragment and the novel is not entirely clear but the fragment was evidently written before Galt had invented his narrator and may well constitute another portion that Galt did not throw into the fire. In the end he incorporated it in Chapter V of the novel. As it quotes in detail from conversations at which the narrator was not present, the interpolation involved Galt in some technical inconsistency which he did not apparently worry too much about.

[9]*Sir Andrew Wylie,* I, 74; III, 300, 307.

[10]Galt is, of course, at pains to stress that Andrew gets on well with people of all classes, with people like his old grandmother and the gypsies just as much as with aristocrats like Lord Sandyford but it is the second kind of connections which pay off.

[11]Professor Gordon explains the narrator's comment as a reference to "Madame Pernelle in *Tartuffe*" (22n) but this strikes me as unlikely. Although Galt would not have needed a specific source for the anecdote, he may well have been reminded of it by R.F. St. Barbe's dramatized version of it in the February 1823 issue of *Blackwood's Magazine* (13, 215-8).

[12]lines 149-150; quoted from *The Poems of Alexander Pope,* ed. John Butt (London: Methuen, 1963), p. 593.

[13]Given Dr. Lounlands' early background, the fact that he speaks English and not Scots may at first sight appear unlikely. Ian Campbell, however, has shown in a detailed examination of a number of nineteenth-century Scottish novels that the clergymen always spoke English and that this situation could, as in the case of Lockhart's Adam Blair, be an important factor in the alienation of the clergyman from the community (See Ian Campbell, *Kailyard* |Edinburgh: Ramsay Head Press, 1981|, Chapter 4). We cannot, of course, assume that a literary convention always faithfully reflects an existing social reality but in this case it seems likely that a substantial connection exists between the two.

[14]|John Galt|, *The Ayrshire Legatees; or, The Pringle Family* (Edinburgh: William Blackwood; London: Cadell, 1821), p. 16.

[15]*The Gathering of the West,* pp. 72-73.

[16]*John Galt: The Life of a Writer,* p. 30.

[17]*Blackwood's Magazine* 8 (February 1821), 502.

[18]*Blackwood's Magazine* 9 (July 1821), 455.

[19]A "potatoe beetle," Professor Gordon tells me (and the *Scottish National Dictionary,* s.v. pitawtie-beetle, confirms) is "a pounder or pestle for mashing cooked potatoes." Hutchesons' Hospital was built by David Hamilton in 1802-5. It is illustrated in A.M. Doak and Andrew McLaren Young (eds.), *Glasgow at a Glance: An Architectural Handbook* (London; Robert Hale, 1977 edition), no. 19.

[20]*The Ayrshire Legatees,* p. 50.

[21]*Blackwood's Magazine* 8 (October 1820), 10-11.

[22]*Blackwood's Magazine* 8 (March 1821), 641; 9 (June 1821), 261.

[23]Adam MacNaughton points out to me that, at least in Ayrshire, a dining-room cupboard is still called a press. What Galt, in spite of the wording, must mean is not that the word had ceased to exist by 1826 but that dining-room cupboards no longer had the same contents as Mrs. Soorocks'. This point is related to a larger question: when is the action of *The Last of the Lairds* supposed to take place? On 1 October 1826 Galt

had written to Moir: "My object in the work was to delineate a set of persons, of his own rank, that such an obsolete character as a West Country Laird was likely, about twenty years ago, to have had for acquaintance and neighbours. . ." (Biographical Memoir," p. xli). The account of Mrs. Soorocks' "press" reinforces the emphasis on the "twenty years ago." On the other hand, as Ian Gordon points out in many of his footnotes, many of the details of the book are very contemporary — Robert Peel's purchase of the Rubens painting already referred to did not take place until 1824, for instance. It would seem that Galt's sense of the right period for the novel shifted as he was writing it and that he was not too concerned with bringing the discrepancies into line.

[24]Coleridge's comment, first printed in 1930, is quoted in Gordon, *John Galt: The Life of a Writer,* pp. 51-52.

[25]See Elizabeth Waterston's essay in this volume, "Bogle Corbet and the Annals of New World Parishes."

[26]*Wuthering Heights* will come to mind as an exception to my statement but the function of its narrators is rather different from what we have in *The Last of the Lairds:* Lockwood is a minor actor at the beginning and at the end and at a few points in the middle but for most of the novel he is like a pane of glass through which Nellie Dean's story is transmitted. Nellie is both the novel's principal narrator and a significant character. She has certainly revalued the characters as well as her own actions but that revaluation took place in the past and is hardly the subject of the novel.

[27]I do not, of course, wish to imply that Ford and Conrad read Galt or were influenced by him. Indeed, it could be argued that, if Galt's experimentation with narrative perspective in *The Last of the Lairds* had been known and understood, there would have been nineteenth-century antecedents to the novels of Ford and Conrad and the development of the nineteenth-century novel would have been rather different.

"Dependents of chance"

Ian Campbell

My title comes from *Bogle Corbet.* Bogle, whose own character as boss and organiser is something we will be considering in our discussion today, very early finds out in Canada that his talents will be needed, when he sees his fellow colonists wavering and divided in their plans for settlement.

> Dependents of chance, they would probably have remained without reflection so long as their wants were supplied, and then they would have scattered themselves, as thoughtless of to-morrow as beasts and birds of prey when they have devoured the carcase. (*B* 74)[1]

It will become obvious in our discussion, I think, that the ordering and regulation of an apparently chaotic society or gathering of individuals is a prevalent theme in Galt's work, and that many of the most popular and enduring features of his fiction arise from his continuing concern for order.

Bogle Corbet is an interesting place to start, not only in light of our Canadian discussion of a Scottish novelist and his work, but from its almost obsessive interest with change and decay. Once the Canadian adventure begins to gain its own momentum, the originally exciting and hopeful gives way to the tedium of the everyday, the accidents of weather and season; the perils of human self-interest intrude on humane consideration and long-range planning. We are given a picture where human settlement succeeds against the odds rather than with them; Elizabeth Waterston reminds us that "we see a reductive spirit at work everywhere."[2] But Margaret Atwood reminds us of another facet of our discussion: the many-layered meanings of survival, ranging from the mere hanging-on to the "vestige of a vanished order which has managed to persist after its time is past, like a primitive reptile."[3] Not an altogether attractive simile: but not everything about being a dependent of chance is very attractive, and one of the enduring fascinations of Galt's work, in Scotland as in Canada, is its realisation of the ambivalence of described experience. A sentence like this is directed exactly at the majority experience of his readers:

> Town-bred people are certainly, of all others, the least fitted to endure with complacency the vicissitudes and privations of a forest-life; and this we experienced to an acute degree. (*B* 122)

Interestingly, the people experiencing are "we," not "they": one of the first things to be noticed about Galt's technique is that it makes a true outsider's viewpoint very hard indeed to sustain. The reader of *Bogle Corbet* is expected to share not one, but two points of view. From the experience of landing in Canada, adjusting to the perils of an extraordinary voyage across the Atlantic and landing on a country which could be the surface of the moon, there is adjustment enough simply to enjoy the novel for vicarious experience. But Bogle is not there for vicarious experience; he has known different times (the character who has known better times, and thus has some kinship with Bogle himself, is a major motif in the story) and has a wider viewpoint than many of the settlers who live just at poverty level, and have little ambition beyond mere survival. And if we let our minds extend to other Galt novels, we recognise the motif: Mrs. Malcolm is attractive to Balwhidder in *Annals of the Parish* becaused she is a genty bodie, someone who has better manners and wider experience (of the city, significantly) than the majority of Dalmailing women. Pawkie makes a good provost because his experience, and his views, are a little — just a little — wider than the townsfolk he manipulates so unblushingly. *The Member* is about someone whose views are wider and whose profit-taking is thus a shameless manipulation of a system he understands a little better than those he milks to his own advantage. And *The Last of the Lairds* is one long and triumphant playing-off of the wider and the narrower view, the Nabob representing (like Cayenne in *Annals of the Parish*) the wider view of the nouveau riche, and the shrewd Scottish good sense representing the local in a very ambivalent view indeed. The local is vanishing fast and the new way is coming fast, but the local can hold out in the hands of an author who sees the attraction of the old way and the full difficulty of adjusting to the new, whether (as in *The Last of the Lairds*) an attempt to hold on grimly, or (*The Entail*) the willingness to sacrifice everything, even human feeling, in a fundamentally useless attempt to hold up the remorseless march of progress.

In *Bogle Corbet* some at least of these problems are already behind the characters. They have, after all, bowed to the inevitable and become dependents of chance by emigrating. Some, like Mrs. Paddock, are outstandingly different, interesting, the "superior" characters whom we have come to recognise as a device by which Galt makes some people stand out for development; many are a chorus of impoverished farmers and small tradesmen. What do they come to ? The answer is a very mixed one.

Campbell of Dungowan, the Highlander, is a case in point; he is one of the "interesting" characters through being given a mysterious past (one, it must be admitted, strained a good deal too much in the rather preposterous coincidences of the plot). Dungowan has material in his possession hidden to the narrator, secrets, as well as the gift of "general good sense" and "gentlemanly demeanour" which "naturally repelled scrutiny" (*B* 98) — and made him an object of interest to Bogle. Dungowan certainly does not make the journey to Canada for worldly advantage: "I only wondered," Bogle sharply observes, "why Dungowan should have been only a Captain; for he had both the talent and tact befitting a higher office." (*ibid.*) His mysterious past covers something serious, and indeed Dungowan is "not much inclined to embark on any business" but encounters Bogle "merely as a visitor. . . and had no particular object in view" (*B* 86). Campbell of Dungowan, in *Bogle Corbet,* finds a country where a little money will go further than it would in Scotland, but he also finds cold, hunger, and inconvenience, to say nothing of his past catching up with him at an uncomfortable moment. He seems happy enough to put his organising talents to Bogle Corbet's use and to take an unquestioned, and unquestioningly superior role in the heirarchy of the new Canadian society. In doing so he echoes two strong motifs which in an earlier discussion[4] I traced in the works of Robert Knowles and his description of Scottish-Canadian Church life at the end of the nineteenth century. One is the willingness of the new Canadian society to accept as natural leaders those who are recent arrivals from Scotland, in precedence to those born in Canada. The other is the continuing willingness of the strong Scottish presbyterian tradition to accept guidance from a respected member of the community, with governmental or Church connection, and work together, particularly when the community is perceived to be one of Scots working together. In these respects Bogle Corbet and Campbell of Dungowan are obvious leaders for the emigrant Scots in Upper Canada: we know that in his own experience in that region Galt worked untiringly for the good of the Scots he found there, and when he wrote in 1827 to the Directors of the Canada Company that "The humble parties with whom I have to traffic supply to me a species of enjoyment, which to many others would perhaps be annoyance,"[5] he was being literally correct. The "species of enjoyment" was the same as Knowles had had in his Canadian ministry, namely the supplying for a body of recent emigrants of a strong controlling force in a new community. For Galt it was both livelihood and source of inspiration and it stored his imagination for both *Lawrie Todd* and *Bogle Corbet.* Both were works which followed on his disgrace and dismissal from Canada, and certainly *Bogle* was written with an "occasional sense of drudgery," not helped by Colburn and Bentley who commissioned a three-volume novel "like an upholsterer. . . a piece of furniture"[6] — with little regard for quality, it seemed to Galt, rather a desire to have a novel the correct length for the correct market. In the circumstances, Galt filled the novel with observations such as those which form the unsatisfactory quasi-*Statistical Account* at the end: the advantage to us seeking a critical insight is that Galt was forced to turn to actual experience to flesh out what he was writing. And actual experience for Galt was the day-to-day administration of the dependents of chance. Small wonder that he found the unusual person interesting (interesting enough to make the basis for a character like Lawrie Todd) when his day-to-day dealings were with the undifferentiated mass of the "humble parties."

We digressed from Campbell of Dungowan to the quality of Galt's daily life in Canada, and the results when rushed down into the print of *Bogle Corbet.* But the overall movement of our discussion is unchanged: we ("we," not "they") are immersed in the description of a new community, and in that we are finding much that is interesting, but some parts more interesting than others, partly for the need of the plot (climax, mystery to be unravelled, incident to relieve mere description or argumentation) and partly because Galt's own memories obviously were concerned less with the mass of those he dealt with daily, than with the exceptions, those who allowed him (to borrow a phrase from Charles Swann) to use "private lives to parallel public events and to show how those events gradually transform a society."[7]

Galt published both in London (*Bogle Corbet*) and in the pages of *Blackwood's,* whether in the bowdlerised but more genteel *Last of the Lairds* which Galt wrote but Moir made fit for the public,[8] or in the large-scale successes which Blackwood cheerfully accepted, *Annals of the Parish, The Ayrshire Legatees, The Provost.* In doing so he was joining the fray for a larger market, beyond the modest rewards of writing just for Scotland. He had seen the astonishing success of Scottish fiction in a national market exemplified by the Author of Waverley: he widened the schema of the Scottish novel in his own practice astonishingly. Our preliminary discussion of *Bogle Corbet* is by no means confined to the conditions Galt knew in Canada; Keith Costain reminds us that

> Galt's new men are frequently called "adventurers" because they are pioneers or explorers seeking their fortune by exciting and daring enterprises, relying for success on such personal qualities as courage or native wit. Their "territory" or "frontier" is the complex modern city or newly established factory town, either of which will be made to serve their purposes much in the way that virgin forest or newly opened prairie serves the purposes of more conventional but similarly motivated pioneers. Mr. Cayenne (who made his capital as a Virginia planter) building a factory town in a once entirely rural area of southwestern Scotland is no less a pioneer than Lawrie Todd. . .[9]

To be a pioneer: to be different, to stand out from the crowd, to make a dream visible and realised, to be part of a public change in private life and realised ambition, to take part and even perhaps to guide in some small way a large change, these things are bases of Galt's plots. Balwhidder is aware of the wish to understand the larger movements of his age, but shrinks from the responsibility and (it has been argued[10]) is made by Galt deliberately unfit for the larger challenge. Jobbry of *The Member* and Provost Pawkie are rather different: they have the larger ambition but are thwarted by their author's desire to rein them in, to make their ambitions larger than their execution, to leave them successful at the local level but thwarted at the larger. They are very like Bogle, whose dreams outrun his ability given the material at hand and the challenges of Upper Canada: his dream fades with every year that the prosperity of his settlement establishes itself, and the new forces (including greed and self-interest) cloud his initial vision. Jobbry (*M* 121)[11] retires from Parliament when he has the native shrewdness to see that he has got everything from being an M.P. that he can — though he cloaks it in his best self-justifying rhetoric, claiming that "my temperate politics were going out of fashion."

In Scotland, as in Canada, Galt saw the challenge of the new and the different, and the real contribution that the understanding of this point makes to our study of Galt the novelist is to underline some of the sources of the control he exercises over the responses to his character. The original definition of this point, by a critic as distinguished as Coleridge, has never been surpassed: it was Coleridge who wrote in his copy of *The Provost* of "the unconscious, perfectly natural, Irony of Self-delusion, in all parts intelligible to the intelligent Reader, without the slightest suspicion on the part of the Autobiographer" (*P*xv).[12] Galt's triumphant achievement is the style of fiction in which narrators again and again betray this unconscious self-delusion. Our discussion can now tie this point in with the material covered so far, as to the ambitions and the frustrations experienced in Galt's fiction by those who are different enough to stand out from the crowd, to be pioneers, to be vulnerable and, often, to be (like their creator) hurt by the imperfect realisation of their dreams.

Galt's first popular success was with *Annals of the Parish:* Rev. Balwhidder has become a favourite public figure with generations who have found in him the embodiment of the white-haired patriarchal Scottish minister, centre of his parish and natural inheritor of information and leadership roles. There are obvious dangers in taking *Annals of the Parish* at this level and this level only. One is to make kailyard of a complicated document, and I have already pointed to the astringency Galt includes in his view of Balwhidder to avoid this very pitfall. Another is to overlook the very obvious derivation of *Annals of the Parish* from the format of the *Statistical Account,* a format popular in Galt's time and practised by him in gathering information on Canada.[13] *Annals of the Parish* would, to readers of his time, be a maze of information to be decoded by the enlightened and interested. Balwhidder's own character would not be one to be accepted passively, but to be measured against the changes he depicts in his narrative. There is a great deal of unconscious self-delusion in Balwhidder, and it is hard for the intelligent reader of *Annals of the Parish* to avoid an affectionate exasperation with his slowness, his lack of vision, his unwillingness to move with the times, indeed to move at all. Many of Balwhidder's parishioners are dependents on chance: the workings of providence are an important motif in the novel[14] and not all of them are benevolent. The press-gang and the sound of distant war are dangerous presences in both the *Annals* and *The Provost.* Balwhidder naturally preaches dependence on Divine Providence, but he notes (1788) "an erect and out-looking spirit abroad that was not to be satisfied with the taciturn regularity of ancient affairs" (*A* 128).[15] Balwhidder prefers the quiet life, the "quiet succession of small incidents" (*A* 100) which characterises most of *Annals of the Parish.* One reason is that Balwhidder, standing apart from his people as a minister must, sees the effects of sudden change after many lifetimes and generations of small incident. In 1794 enlistment to the army was commonplace, and

> I could not help remarking to myself, that the people were grown so used to changes and extraordinary adventures, that the single enlistment of Thomas Wilson, at the beginning of the American war, occasioned a far greater grief and work among us, than all the swarms that went off week after week in the months of November and December of this year. (*A* 148)

There are advantages to being in Dalmailing, where "in the clachan we lived in the lea of the dike" (*A* 176), including having a wider vision than those close up to the seat of the action. Balwhidder cannot comprehend the French Revolution (*A* 139) nor (much more importantly) the change brought to his parish by the arrival of a bookshop aimed specifically not at the gentry and the ministers, but at the new proletariat of the millworkers (*A* 133-4), yet he is at least free from fashions and fads, and in his own limited way can preach to a people whose vision is almost as limited as his own. As minister he is *a little* ahead of his flock, but Lord Eaglesham and Mr. Cayenne are far ahead of Balwhidder, men of wider vision and wider experience, men used by Galt to pinpoint and highlight the limitations of the narrator himself. Yet, cleverly, Balwhidder can score a few points: when put to it in Edinburgh he can (almost by mistake) score an immense success in his General Assembly sermon, and when he has to he can, through peasant shrewdness, give excellent advice to the worldly Mr. Cayenne when the latter is stalled (*A* 177). Like Bogle Corbet in Canada he is a man who gains a few, loses a few; ahead of his wife in some things, he is put in his place by her in others. Bogle is superior to his emigrant band — certainly in interpreting their fate to them — but he has a lot to learn and (his creator would ruefully admit) a man can make mistakes in trying to colonise Upper Canada.

A man can go only so far: it is the *Leitmotiv* of much of Galt's fiction, set in both Scotland and Canada. Quite apart from taking on Providence or Chance, a man has enough ado to take on the circumstances of the everyday which Galt makes his peculiar providence. The Coleridgeian eye noted the self-delusion *quite invisible* to the person concerned: in *The Ayrshire Legatees* Dr. Pringle is quite blind to the pomposity and the old-fashioned view of the ministry which makes him a figure of gentle fun even in Garnock where he is loved and reverenced by most. But this manipulation of points of view is really Galt's best point in his novel: trapped in Garnock, Pringle is perfectly happy. But chance throws him into the wider world: not the destitution which uprooted Bogle Corbet, but an enormous inheritance which means the Pringles have to go to London and undergo a comic series of incidents and opportunities of seeing the wider world there. And the net result is a peculiarly interesting one. Of course there is the opportunity for a good deal of fun at the expense of the Scottish provincials, and as we would expect from Galt a good deal of fun is made of the Londoners at the same time. But the most surprising result of this wider experience I have already suggested is the most unexpected possible:[16] once outside his narrow field, Pringle sees that he cannot go back and settle to being a country minister with a fortunate inheritance of £100,000 and more in the bank — for human nature would simply not admit of unconscious self-delusion on this scale. Once out, Pringle cannot re-enter Garnock on these terms even though Garnock seems more than happy to have its minister back, thronging round him in Church like Balwhidder's parishioners (*A* 277)[17] and declaring public holidays just to see the minister and his wife come home in the extreme novelty of their own coach and horses (*AL* 266). Pringle has the sense to see through his own previous imperfections, and to retire rapidly to a country house existence (*AL* 279) leaving the parish in the hands of a younger, more flexible minister who has *some* wider experience (Edinburgh, the novels of Scott) but not so much as Pringle, now a Londoner and man of the world. Just so much experience is enough for the minister of Garnock: Galt's comic message is quite plain. The end of *The Ayrshire Legatees* is typical of Galt's complex analysis of his society. People are happy again, but not with the *status quo,* rather with something which has been re-tailored given the new experience of the people concerned. Providence's workings are accepted, but some re-adjustment of human values to providence's is expected.

Just this same complexity attends the end of *The Provost.* Pawkie has had a good innings running the affairs of Gudetown and milking the position for everything he can to his own advantage. Providence has come and Pawkie has taken Providence in his stride — though how we look on Pawkie as a result is not easy to be sure.

> I think upon the whole, however, that our royal burgh was not afflicted to any very dangerous degree [by the radical spirit of the French Revolution], though there was a sort of itch of it among a few of the sedentary orders, such as the weavers and shoemakers, who, by the nature of sitting long in one posture, are apt to become subject to the flatulence of theoretical opinions. . . [but] I kept a steady eye on the proceedings of the ministers and parliament at London, taking them for an index and model for the management of the public concerns. . .(*P* 57-8)

Now, when we consider that the story of Pawkie's management of the concerns of Gudetown is one of shameless jobbery, manipulation, profit-taking and bribery, this reflects in a very complicated way (as we always expect from Galt) — against Pawkie, and against the London government on which he claims to model himself. Of course there is also a measure of self-irony in this, for Pawkie models himself on something distant he barely understands. What he *does* understand (like Jobbry in *The Member*) is the principle of making a penny for himself at every turn in the public business. After the riots of Gudetown are put down with his help Pawkie notices that

> I had (and why should I disguise the honest fact) my share of the advantage which the

kingdom at large drew, in that period of anarchy and confusion, from the laudable establishment of a volunteer force. (*P* 65).

In exactly the same way Jobbry thinks it no shame to admit that "my share of patronage" was "one of the principal inducements which led me originally to think it advisable to go into Parliament" (*M* 101). Pawkie shares with Jobbry, and with Dr. Pringle from *The Ayrshire Legatees,* the very good sense to know when he has gone as far as he can: Balwhidder has the knowledge forced on him, and in *The Last of the Lairds* Malachi Mailing almost by accident has the knowledge put in front of him by the plot and by the other characters. *Self* knowledge in these Galt novels come slowly and painfully, but it comes with experience and the interworking of personal destiny with the larger concerns of the plot, national interest, personal and societal change, political and military history and — to return to the reason for the Guelph Conference on Galt — the interplay between Galt's own travels abroad, particularly to Canada, and the acute Scottish experience which was the groundwork for most of the realistic fiction we are considering here.

We began with the realisation that Bogle Corbet thought he had a mission to guide and give shape to the destinies of those "Dependents of Chance" whom he found as emigrants in Upper Canada, and we know he was keenly interested by their affairs, and returned home to Britain with a keen memory of their day-to-day experience, as well as of the outstanding people (Tiger Wull Dunlop, for instance, and the original of Lawrie Todd) and events (the memorable description of the cutting of the first tree for the site of the future city of Guelph) of his Canadian years. He himself, through his exertions and his superior powers of observation and administration, had taken on the forces of chance — and his experience made it unlikely that he would have a simplistic or sentimental approach. Nor had he; *Bogle Corbet,* like *Lawrie Todd,* is about the frustrations and shortcomings of the colonisation experience fully as much as about the challenge and the satisfaction. But the intention of this discussion has been to make a bridge between this effect and a narrative method central to Galt's success, namely the author's manipulation of narrative stances from the perceiving core of the novel. A Galt narrator also experiences shortcomings and frustrations in living and depicting his ideal world. Some characters like Jobbry or Pawkie would like to conquer the available world and make themselves Nabob, but their native shrewdness makes them recognise their native limitation, and they pose no threat to the reader since they rein themselves back. Other characters, like Mailing and Pringle, are less self-aware and it is left to the other characters, and to the convolutions of the plot, to bring them up to the barriers which circumscribe their ambition. Most complex, and most successful, is Balwhidder in *Annals of the Parish.* He sees least of his own imperfection, but his ambitions are closest to those the audience can approve. He recognises and co-operates with a divine chance which affects human life on a local and engaging plane — while dimly perceiving the wider changes and chances of a society known to Galt readers, and implied even if not fully perceived by the slow wits of a country patriarch. Balwhidder is too slow, and too provincial, to have either the manic ambitions of a Jobbry or a Pawkie, or the restless itch and the manipulative skill of a Bogle Corbet.

But finally Bogle Corbet is only allowed by his creator to go so far. His own manipulative ambitions are soon cut short by the facts of life and his restless itch is cramped by poor roads, appalling climate, and a very realistically-observed family position. He must compromise continually between what, theoretically, he would like to be able to do, and what that formidable matriarch Mrs. Corbet will sanction, and the various accidents of domestic responsibility permit. *Bogle Corbet* the novel is pitched not to present a Utopian dream of Canada, but to interpret the fallible experiences of one narrator who is as quizzically observed as Pawkie or Balwhidder. Bogle's amibitions lie in

> faithfully reciting the progress of my own course, to afford to those who may follow, something like the instruction furnished by example. The poor emigrant must, I fear, still struggle with neglect; but those, the few and rare, who happen to possess some means, and who are competent to render information available — which is not always in the power of the best-educated to do — may possibly derive hints from this narrative that will not be useless. (*B* 31)

Even the best-educated cannot necessarily write prescriptively and successfully: Bogle does not claim to be either best-educated or to write the definitive guide to Canada. And it has been the purpose of this discussion to suggest that the strengths of Galt's achievement in fiction like this lie in the limitations both of his intention, and his narrative *persona.* To derive hints from a narrative like this, and to have each reader translate such information into a form suitable to local circumstance and personal opinion, was the achievement which brought Galt in his own time a good measure of popular success, and which still gives him the power to be a popular Scottish novelist with a range as narrow as the parish pump of Dalmailing, and as wide as the workings of Chance in the dangerous forests of Upper Canada.

NOTES

[1]John Galt, *Bogle Corbet* ed. E. Waterston (Toronto: McClelland and Stewart, 1977), 74.

[2]*Op.cit.,* introduction, 6.

[3]M. Atwood, *Survival: a thematic guide to Canadian literature* (Toronto: Anansi, 1972), 32.

[4]"John Galt and the Kailyard," *Scottish tradition* 11-12 (1981-2), 163-177.

[5]J. Aberdein, *John Galt,* (London: Oxford, 1936), 155.

[6]I.A. Gordon, *John Galt, The life of a writer* (Toronto: University of Toronto, 1972), 101.

[7]Charles Swann, "Past into present: Scott, Galt and the historical novel," *Literature and history* 3 (March, 1976), 69.

[8]I.A. Gordon, "Plastic surgery on a nineteenth-century novel: John Galt, William Blackwood, Dr. D.M. Moir and *The last of the lairds,*" *The Library* 32 (1977), 246-55.

[9]K.M. Costain, "The spirit of the age and the Scottish fiction of John Galt," *The Wordsworth circle* (Spring, 1980), 102.

[10]In Ian Campbell, *Kailyard: a new assessment* (Edinburgh: Ramsay Head Press, 1981), 48-55.

[11]John Galt, *The member: an autobiography* ed. I.A. Gordon (Edinburgh: Scottish Academic Press, 1975).

[12]John Galt, *The provost* ed. I.A. Gordon (London: Oxford, 1973).

[13]Ian Campbell, "John Galt's annals of his parish, 1760-1810." forthcoming in the *Proceedings of the Scottish colloquium, 1984,* Old Dominion University, Norfolk, Va.

[14]See an important discussion in John MacQueen, "John Galt and the analysis of soctial history," *Scott bicentenary essays* ed. A. Bell (Edinburgh: Scottish Academic Press, 1973), 332-42.

[15]John Galt, *Annals of the parish* ed. J. Kinsley (London: Oxford, 1967).

[16]Ian Campbell, "Town and country: *The Ayrshire legatees,*" in *John Galt 1779-1979* ed. C.A. Whatley (Edinburgh: Ramsay Head, 1979), 92-106.

[17]John Galt, *The Ayrshire legatees* ed. D.S. Meldrum, introduction by S.R. Crockett (Edinburgh: Blackwood, 1895).

Galt and politics

Ian A. Gordon

There are two John Galts. Sometimes they merge. Generally, they are kept well apart. There is, first, the John Galt of *Annals of the Parish,* the faithful recorder of a vanishing past, an eighteenth century rural Scotland that was disappearing even while he wrote about it; a writer with a love of the expressive west-country dialect of the region in which he had been brought up; the author of half a dozen novels to which he gave the collective title *Tales of the West.*

The author of the *Annals,* of *The Entail, The Provost* and *The Last of the Lairds* is a major Scottish novelist.

There is another John Galt, the eager young businessman hoping to make his fortune in London, the resolute European voyager and fellow-traveller with Lord Byron, the parliamentary lobbyist who assiduously hung around the corridors of power, nursing bills through parliament where — in his own words — he had "upwards of sixty acquaintances, members of parliament." He spent years of his life getting to know what he deemed to be the right people, those who had votes or influence or power; all the while nursing a secret ambition to be himself well-off and powerful.

This second John Galt was familiar with men (and women) of titled rank. He was presented at Court. The King spoke to him. He equipped himself, as a young man, with "a new seal with armorial bearings." The King was graciously pleased to receive volumes "bound in the royal manner" of several of his books and to accept the dedications to two of them. This second John Galt, the busy, ambitious man of affairs, did not write in the Scottish dialect. He wrote, and wrote very effectively, the King's English.

Galt never let his right hand know what his left hand was up to. Or rather, he did not let the public image of himself, which he cultivated carefully, of the shrewd organiser and puller of wires, the canny Scot who could get things done — he did not let this public image ever be confused in public with his alter ego, the writer who could settle down for weeks at a time in a quiet room, turning out page after page, often without a word of correction, of imaginative fiction and memorable character creation.

Only a few people write autobiographies. Galt is unusual, if not unique, in having provided us with not one but with two. He produced in 1833 a massive two-volume work entitled *The Autobiography of John Galt,* dedicated to one of his senior parliamentary helpers, the Right Honourable Edward Ellice, M.P., then Secretary at War. Amid those hundreds of pages devoted to Galt's public activities in London and in Canada there are only three short chapters, amounting to a mere twenty pages, on his literary work. The *Autobiography* is intended as the story of John Galt, the public figure. A year later he published a second autobiography in a single volume of over 350 pages. He did not call it an autobiography. He called it *The Literary Life of John Galt* and he dedicated it (with royal permission) to the King, whom he had come to regard as his literary patron.

During the great part of his working career, Galt went to great pains to keep these two lives — of the literary man and the man of affairs — severely separate, at least in the mind of the public. He would not have his name on the title-pages of his fine Scottish novels. His *The Ayrshire Legatees* made an anonymous appearance in instalments in *Blackwood's Edinburgh Magazine.* The first of his novels to be published in book form (in April 1821) was *Annals of the Parish.* It bore no author's name. Two months later *The Ayrshire Legatees* came out as a separate book. Its title-page tells you it is "By the Author of Annals of the Parish." *Sir Andrew Wylie* of 1822 is similarly "By the Author of Annals of the Parish." *The Provost,* which came out later in the year, is "By the Author of Annals of the Parish, Ayrshire Legatees, and Sir Andrew Wylie." His major novel *The Entail* of late 1822 was, technically speaking, anonymous, identified only by the authorship claimed on the title-page of earlier and by now well-known books. Even his final novel of the *Tales of the West* sequence, *The Last of the lairds* of 1826, by which date Galt was well established as a novelist with the critical journals of the day openly writing of his achievement, is "By the author of Annals of the Parish, The Entail, etc." Nowhere in this sequence of well-known novels is there any hint of the author's name.

He could not keep his authorship secret. Indeed the author, John Galt number one (as I propose to call him in this paper) took a great deal of pleasure — and who could blame him? — in reading commendations of his work in the journals of the day. But that public figure — whom I shall call John Galt number two — insisted that his name should not appear on his title-pages nor, if possible, even in advertisements for his novels. When the Edinburgh firm of Oliver and Boyd were about to publish one of his historical tales in December 1823 he wrote firmly to Boyd "I wish my name as little brought in as possible. You know my parliamentary concerns, and some folk are apt to think that business may be neglected by and for the vanities of authorship."

Galt had a high regard for each side of his activity. But he had different expectations from each. From his novel-writing he hoped for reputation and some modest income. From his public activities he hoped for something much more solid. His quest for a literary reputation must never be allowed to get in the way of his pursuit of a reasonable fortune. *He* knew that novel writing was a serious business; he also knew that the hard-headed politicians with whom he had to deal held it in little regard. For them it was mere vanity.

As his reputation as a novelist grew, he had a further reason for insisting that his title-pages carried merely some such indicator as "By the Author of Annals of the Parish." Galt wrote with a Defoe-like verisimilitude and his best writing is all in the first person. He did not wish the "I" of his various novels to be confused with himself. Those personalities whose thoughts and language he so skilfully adopted were not to be thought of as John Galt. The danger of confusion was a real one — William Blackwood's old mother was bitterly disappointed to find that *Annals of the Parish* was a novel. She had read it as the reminiscences of a real clergyman!

Galt had a remarkable ability to assume a *persona* in writing. He had the real novelist's ability to get inside the skin of a character. This brought him literary fame. It also brought misunderstandings. Galt was not what the Scots of his day would have called a god-fearing man. He was basically secular and I have some doubts that he regarded himself as a Christian. Certainly, in his final days, when a visiting clergyman pressed him to declare his Christian beliefs, Galt remained obdurately silent. When the minister further pressed him, offering him "divine mercy," Galt's reply was that he was planning his summer holidays — and bystanders were convinced that he was making fun of the minister. This was the man who had created the Reverend Micah Balwhidder, like the Vicar of Wakefield regarded as the epitome of simple Christian faith!

In *Ringan Gilhaize* he similarly created a god-fearing Covenanter, faithfully reproducing his biblical language and his rebellious anti-government attitudes. He sent two copies of the finished novel to the Home Secretary, Sir Robert Peel, one copy for Peel and the second for possible presentation to the King. Galt in his covering letter carefully dissociated himself from the views of his covenanting hero. "I am anxious not to have it imputed to me that, in condemnation of the policy of the Stuarts, I feel less faithfully attached to the existing Government." Peel reassured him. The King got his copy and Sir Robert in his reply wrote that he was flattered to receive a volume from an author whose previous works he had "perused with so much interest and gratification."

In this exchange with Sir Robert Peel the two Galts for once seem to merge. John Galt number one (who to the end of his days always regarded *Ringan Gilhaize* as his best novel) is justifiably pleased with his performance and offers tentatively yet another royal copy. John Galt number two is making a useful contact with a Minister of State and ensuring that his public image is that of a staunch government supporter whose sympathetic portrayal of a rebel must be read for what it is, a piece of creative fiction. Galt is trying to get the best of both his personalities and in this instance manages to succeed.

My brief today is to discuss Galt's involvement with politics. It is an invitation I have accepted with pleasure. But which John Galt was involved? Was it Galt the novelist or Galt the public figure? The reason for my long introduction is to establish that there really were two John Galts and though each of them was involved in politics, the involvement, and the ultimate results, were totally different.

Let us take the more obvious first, the figure I call John Galt number two. When he settled in London and married he was already a writer and had dabbled in business. An opportunity arose to supervise an export venture and for this he had to return to Scotland. But — as he said — "the scheme ended in smoke" and he returned to London "to write for the periodicals." Some of the Scottish entrepreneurs, however, had been impressed by his ability and his obvious knowledge of who was who in London. The Edinburgh and Glasgow Union Canal Company needed to get a private bill through parliament and they appointed Galt their agent for the assignment. It took him a couple of sessions but he canvassed M.P.s. diligently (in his own ironical words his conduct was "saponaceous"). The bill passed, and the Canal Company rewarded Galt "handsomely." It was to be the first of several assignments of the same type.

Galt never became a politician in the accepted sense of the word, but over the next few years he came to know parliamentary personalities and parliamentary procedures with a great deal of intimacy. He knew his way around and acquired a growing reputation as a skilful and resourceful negotiator. The ultimate result was to be one of his best novels. But that lay well in the future. The more immediate outcome was involvement with Canadian affairs.

Here, in this city of Guelph which Galt founded, I tread with caution. I have, as you are aware, written a biography of Galt, carefully subtitled "The Life of a Writer." It was published by the University of Toronto. The Galt on whom I wrote my book is John Galt number one, not John Galt number two. I think I can claim to have seen all the documents that matter on the life and activities of Galt the writer. They are mostly in Britain, though I did get some large reels of microfilm from the National Archives in Ottawa. In spite of the University of Toronto imprint, my book on Galt, and my first-hand knowledge, is confined to Galt the writer, not Galt as a Canadian founding father.

For this reason, as I say, I tread carefully. My knowledge of Canadian history is necessarily second-hand and I have, for much of the story, only what you might call Galt's word for it. There may well be other points of view and documents that I know not of. Here is what I understood from what I have read.

When America declared war on Britain in 1812 and moved troops across the Canadian border many settlers in Upper Canada suffered losses. At the end of hostilities they looked for compensation and they looked to the Colonial Office in London. Much to Galt's surprise he was approached and then appointed their agent in London. His fee would depend on his success and he set about the job with his usual vigour. After four years of lobbying and politicking he had gained nothing for the settlers but he had gained a considerable interest in Canadian affairs and in the prospect of a great commercial enterprise opening up the forests of Upper Canada. He looked around for venture capitalists who would establish a Canada Company. It was formed in 1824 with Galt as secretary. The following year Galt and four other commissioners (none of whom had seen the land they were investing money in) made a visit of inspection of some months. On their return Galt was appointed Superintendent of the Company's affairs in Upper Canada, arriving back in Ontario towards the end of 1826, to throw himself with characteristic energy into the task. His old dream, of controlling a vast business enterprise, had at last come true and in later life he always remembered 1827 as "the most active year of my whole life." Less than three years later, he was back in England, recalled by the Company.

I shall not attempt to recount the details. From all appearances, Galt did a first-rate job. Towns were founded. Guelph is one of them. Surveys were conducted and explorations mounted. Roads were built. Settlers were established on the land; all under Galt's supervision and with his active encouragement. He seems on the face of it to have done all the right things. Yet for Galt (though not for Canada) the whole operation came unstuck. From the outset he met little but opposition from local government circles. The authorities in Lower Canada regarded him with suspicion because of his earlier involvement as agent for the disgruntled settlers. The Lieutenant-Governor of Upper Canada suspected Galt (a life-long middle class Tory) of radical sympathies. I think what finally brought about his downfall was the length in these days of the lines of communication. The London directors of the Company wanted reports and they wanted quick financial returns on their capital. Galt was the man on the spot. He had to make decisions and make them off the cuff. If a group of destitute settlers arrived he felt he had to feed them, house them before the winter set in, put the able-bodied among them to work on his new roads. It seemed to make sense. But London heard of these things after a delay of months and finally they panicked, withdrew Galt's authorisation to incur expenditure and simply recalled him. Galt had no option. He sailed for Liverpool. What he called his "philanthropic dream" was for him all over.

Does this make Galt a failed politician? He certainly knew that he had failed and his later *Autobiography* is a long apologia. What I find ironic is that so many of his decisions seem to have turned out to be correct. Others, eventually, reaped where he had sowed — including (fortunately) his three sons, who contributed so much to Canada. As I see it, Galt had all the ability that was required and three times the energy. What he was never given was the authority and the public status required. Had he arrived, fitted out (say) with the K.C.M.G. that his youngest son was later to acquire, who knows how far he might have gone? It is idle speculation. Galt was out of a job. His creditors swooped, considering him now a bad risk, and he spent four months of 1829 in the debtors' prison of the King's Bench. In his own words he "retired from the arena of business with the sullenness of a vanquished bull."

It was the end of John Galt number two. It was not the end by any means of John Galt. What emerged from the prison of the King's Bench was the real hero of my story, John Galt number one.

From the time he was a young man Galt was fascinated by politics. By "politics" I do not mean the day to day struggle between political parties. "Politics" meant to Galt something more academic, the area of study now called in some quarters political science. When he first arrived in London he had time on his hands and he devoted a great deal of it to reading. He read widely in the classics of political theory and political economy (as it was then called), from Machiavelli down to the writers of his own day. In all this he was guided by a friend he had made in London, the learned Dr. Alexander Tilloch, who owned and edited an evening political newspaper *The Star* and who also edited a serious-minded heavyweight periodical *The Philosophical Magazine.* In it Galt saw his first serious political article published, and essay on *Commercial Policy.*

A year or so later, in 1812, Galt launched out into a fuller exposition of his views on political theory in a booklet of 100 pages. Since there appears to be only one extant copy, it is unlikely that you will have seen it. Let me at least give you its full title: *Cursory Reflections on Political and Commercial Topics as connected with the Regent's Accession to the Royal Authority.* This publication demonstrates Galt fascinated by the exercise of political power and of decision-making in a modern state. It is the kind of well-written and intelligent analysis that many universities would now happily accept as a Master's dissertation: Galt thinking cogently on the political issues of his day. When this kind of philosophical background was, within a few years, to be combined with a first-hand knowledge of the actual mechanism of parliament, Galt had only to add his flair for characterisation and he was ready to produce political novels.

We do not usually think of Galt as a political novelist. Yet a political novelist he was, and on more than one occasion. *The Provost* of 1822 was on its first appearance a success. The initial edition of 2000 was sold off in a fortnight and *Blackwood's Magazine* reported with delight that the second edition was melting away "like snaw aff a dike." It sold for the obvious reason: it was a richly comic book. Galt was continuing to provide his public with the brand of Scottish country humour they had come to expect of the author of *Annals* and *The Ayrshire Legatees.*

Yet *The Provost* is more than a collection of Scots comedy characters and scenes. It is a close piece of observation, a shrewd analysis of the exercise of political power. It is true that the operation is conducted within a small community, in the town council of a self-governing Scottish burgh. Galt saw with clarity that political manipulation is the same, whether it is exercised in the council-room of his native town of Irvine or in the more spacious Chamber of Westminister. The difference lay only in the scale of the operation and the size of the sums involved. The "principles" were the same. Provost Pawkie speedily learns how "to rule without being felt, which is the true mystery of policy." He knew when to act, when to drag his feet and bide his time, whom to flatter, whom to bribe, whom to manipulate in or out of office. Pawkie slyly confesses that he was soon able "to wind the council round my finger." He had never heard of Machiavelli. He had no need to. His creator had.

I put out a fully-annotated edition of *The Provost* in the *Oxford English Novels* series some years ago. Like Galt's own first edition it went out of print (Galt still sells). It has recently been reprinted as a paperback in the *World's Classics* series and this has brought it to the attention of a wider range of readers. To me one of the most interesting things about the reviews has been the ready recognition that this is not only a funny book but is also a serious political study. "Nobody," says Marghanita Laski in a full-page review, "who has ever had anything to do with voluntary public service at whatever level, can fail to recognise with glee the machinations, the manoeuvres, the sheer cunning. . . The provost's times are singularly like our own." Provost Pawkie's world (says the *Times Literary Supplement*) "has a timeless air." Let me turn to a reviewer in a small paper in New York State – "Politics has altered so little in the intervening centuries that readers today will have little difficulty recognizing contemporary figures in this subtle and ironic portrait of a professional political manipulator." I am not the only one to see Galt as a first-rate political novelist. *The Provost* was his first political novel.

While he was writing *The Provost* Galt was simultaneously engaged on a further political novel, designed as a companion piece. Galt's intention was to do a parallel study, this time of a "humble Scotchman" who made his way to London, progressed there in the law, made a favourable impression on an earl and his countess, to be given (in those pocket borough days) a seat in parliament. There his shrewd outspoken comments were heard only in committee, never on the public platform. His reward was a baronetcy and a triumphal return to Scotland. Sir Andrew Wylie was to be a very different kind of political animal from James Pawkie. He was meant to be the kind of politician that I think Galt admired, the party man loyal in public who behind the scenes was yet a powerful moderating force on the more retrograde aspects of party policy.

His first draft turned out to be longer than *The Provost.* Galt thought it might need two volumes. His publisher William Blackwood had other ideas. Recognising that Galt had run beyond his usual one-volume length, he saw the chance to get from him one of the then fashionable three-volume extended novels so much in request from the subscription libraries. He demanded expansion, "a good and striking story" replacing Galt's normal episodic method. Galt was unwilling but – to his lasting regret – capitulated. The ultimate *Sir Andrew Wylie* of 1822 is replete with complex plotting and incidents which Galt later was to condemn as "too romantic and uncommon for my taste."

I have discussed elsewhere in detail the sad tale of the re-writing of this novel, and shall not repeat myself here. My reason for including *Sir Andrew Wylie* at this point was to show that in Galt's original plan it was conceived as his second political novel, a deliberate companion piece to *The Provost.* Even in its present form, the political chapters are most effective. We have to add Sir Andrew to Galt's gallery of politicians. There will be more to come.

The decline of John Galt number two had been, as we have seen, dramatic. At one moment he was a kind of pro-consul, in charge of a vast territory. A few months later he was incarcerated for insolvency in the King's Bench prison for debtors. At this point John Galt number one took over. His wife and three sons were still in Canada. When he finally gained his discharge under the Insolvent Act at the end of 1829, he had to find some means of supporting himself and his family and he returned to his pen. One of his fellow-writers describes him at this time working at his desk "in dour silence and imperturbable stoicism."

He poured out articles for the periodicals, *Blackwood's, Fraser's The New Monthly Magazine,* the *National Standard,* any journal that would print him and pay him. He returned to novel-writing. The novels he wrote in the course of the next year or so were pure pot-boilers, rapidly written three-deckers for the firm of Colburn and Bentley who (as Galt said) ordered novels as if they were ordering upholstery. Galt was under no illusions. He wrote in his later *Autobiography* that he "would not wish to be estimated" by these Colburn and Bentley commissioned pieces of upholstery.

He adopted a curious way of signalling that he was writing second-rate fiction under duress. He signed all his Colburn and Bentley novels with his own name! It is an odd reversal of the more usual practice of writing one's best things under one's own name and pieces written merely for quick cash under a nom de plume. But all of Galt's novels on which his literary reputation had been established were written under a nom de plume — "The Author of The Ayrshire Legatees," "The Author of Annals of the Parish, etc.," in other words John Galt number one. In openly signing his name to these Colburn and Bentley novels Galt was signalling in his own private code that the writer was that well-known public figure who had been publicly declared insolvent and who was frankly in need of the money. The Colburn and Bentley pot-boilers arose from the immediate needs of John Galt number two.

Towards the end of 1831 Galt could see his way out of the woods. His old friends, such as Ellice and the faithful Lockhart, had rallied round. The stock of the Canada Company rose and (though Galt had no hopes of re-engagement) he saw himself rehabilitated in the public eye. "I saw that I might again go among my old friends, without blushing for an undertaking, the solidity of which had been vindicated." He set himself to throw off the shackles of Colburn and Bentley and returned to the writing of proper novels.

That they were novels of the kind he really wanted to write and knew that he could write well is clear to anyone who recognises his private code; they are by John Galt number one. His next two novels (which appeared in close succession in January and in May 1832) signal his intentions. The title-page of the first bears no author's name. The novel (*The Member*) is "By the Author of The Ayrshire Legatees etc. etc." The second novel (*The Radical*) is "By the Author of The Member, The Ayrshire Legatees, etc. etc." Both are short one-volume productions; both are "autobiographies", the author assuming the persona of a fictional hero. John Galt number one was back in business.

Both these novels are political novels. While Galt was engaged in writing them, political reform was in the air in Westminster and throughout the country. The Reform Bill would be passed in 1832 and Britain would take its first step towards a full franchise with every adult a voter. Galt's sensitive political antennae reacted, and in these two novels, *The Member* and *The Radical,* he created a couple of politicians who represent the two sides of the debate that preceded the passing of the Reform Bill.

The Member combines Galt's deep knowledge of rural Scotland with his intimate acquaintance with the House of Commons. The hero Archibald Jobbry is a Scot who has returned a wealthy nabob after service with the East Indian Company. Finding himself surrounded by impoverished kinsmen he decides that the best way of meeting their demands is to enter parliament, from which he can dispense patronage and to him costless favours. He buys a seat in a rotten borough and once he is in the House his shrewd amalgam of party loyalty and jaunty self-assurance makes him courted by Ministers. As times goes on, his views alter; he discovers that he "has lost something of the relish" in political manipulation. As a "moderate Tory", opposed to the radical element, he yet finds himself out of sympathy with the "real Tories of the House" and gradually comes to see Reform as inevitable. He decides to retire and sell his seat — only to find it is unsellable since the Reform Bill has abolished his constituency. It is a brilliantly ironical study of political activity written by a man who knew what he was talking about.

The Member was welcomed by the reviewers of Galt's day. They recognised that the old Galt had returned. *The Athenaeum* wished "Mr. Galt would do nothing but write imaginary autobiographies." For reasons I have fully discussed elsewhere *The Member* did not go into a second edition and it was not included in the various collected editions of Galt's works. A few copies have survived on library shelves. In 1975 I brought out an annotated edition. It, too, is now out of print (I did say that Galt sells).

As with a recent edition of *The Provost,* the reviews of this edition have stressed Galt's universality: his unerring eye and ear for what seems permanent in political dealings. The *Times Literary Supplement* found the old 1832 *The Member* had in 1975 "a startling topicality." It was reviewed in one of the weeklies by Jo Grimmond, then the leader of the British Liberal Party and a Member of Parliament of twenty-five years' standing. He found it a disquieting book. After a century and a half of continuing "Reform" culminating in universal suffrage, Galt's picture of political manipulation and rewards remained accurate for the 1970s. Only the labels had changed. "Mr. Jobbry would have been profoundly envious of the patronage now dispensed by governments and their civil servants." *Plus ca change plus c'est la même chose.* Galt in his short career as a practical politician had no great success. As a political theorist and political observer he had a happy knack of getting to the heart of the matter.

The Member was followed by *The Radical.* It was never reprinted and still awaits a second edition. To find a copy you must hunt it down in a major research library. I shall therefore give it only brief attention. Its hero Nathan Butt is, like Archibald Jobbry, a Member of Parliament in the year before the passing of the Reform Bill. He is no sooner elected than he is expelled from his seat on the grounds that his election involved perjury. The reader never actually meets him in a parliamentary setting. Galt had thoroughly explored that setting in *The Member* and had no wish to repeat himself. What Galt presents instead is a case-history of the kind of politician now often known as a left-winger. Nathan Butt is the natural rebel. He is expelled from school and his education is completed by reading not the past classics of political theory but Rousseau's *Social Contract,* William Godwin's *Caleb Williams* and *Political Justice* – the "revolutionary" books of his time. Nathan Butt is, in the terminology of his day, a Radical. . . and Galt (who was no radical) portrays him with sympathy and understanding.

These two books brought Galt's career as a novelist to a close. He fell ill and within a couple of years had left the London scene. In retreat in Scotland, he continued to write. The novel was beyond him. He sent in some admirable short stories to the periodicals. I collected the best of these together in my 1978 volume Galt's *Selected Short Stories.* I find it significant that the last story he ever published, in the December 1836 issue of *Fraser's Magazine* was a political one entitled *The Statesman.* It is a mocking and ironical manual on the manipulation of political power. Galt's interest in politics remained with him to the end.

I conclude with a word of warning. If you are reading Galt's political novels, do not commit the error of William Blackwood's old mother. Do not confuse their central figures with John Galt. He had his own political views. They were not those of his political characters. In the five works I have discussed he offered a whole spectrum: the scheming successful politician who always contrives to fall on his feet; the good party man who is yet not a mere sycophant; the good party man who has the courage to change his mind and move with the times; the born rebel who will always be in opposition even when his own party is in power; and the statesman, which is simply another name for a political survivor. Galt knew them all. When the history of the political novel comes to be written, pride of place must go to Galt. He was its initiator; and in his two best political novels, *The Provost* and *The Member,* he was (as he had been in his best Scottish novels) a writer of formidable talent. I welcome this opportunity to commend him in this the city of Guelph which he founded.